GOD'S
ARMORBEARER
How To Serve God's Leaders

GOD'S ARMORBEARER
How To Serve God's Leaders

by
Terry Nance

Unless otherwise indicated, all Scripture quotations are taken from the *King James Version* of the Bible.

Scriptures quotations marked *AMP* are taken from *The Amplified Bible*, Old Testament. Copyright © 1962, 1964 by Zondervan Publishing House, Grand Rapids, Michigan.

10 09   45 44 43 42 41 40 39 38 37 36 35 34

GOD'S ARMORBEARER: How To Serve God's Leaders
ISBN 978-0-9719193-2-7
Copyright © 1990 by Terry Nance

Published by Focus on the Harvest
P.O. Box 6655
Sherwood, AR 72124

Dedication

This book is lovingly dedicated to my mom, Jean Nance, a godly woman of love, prayer and faithfulness.

Special thanks to Mike Camacho for the research material which he provided me on the word *armorbearer*.

Contents

Foreword

1 Revelation of an Armorbearer   11

2 Function of an Armorbearer   17

3 Armorbearers of the Old Testament   33

4 New Testament Armorbearing   43

5 The Cry of God's Leaders   55

6 How to Develop the Spirit of an Armorbearer   61

Foreword

He that delicately bringeth up his servant from a child shall have him become his son at the length (Prov. 29:21).

This scripture accurately describes the spiritual relationship between Terry Nance and myself.

As Terry gave himself to God for the fulfilling of his calling, the ministry of a true armorbearer came forth and blossomed.

This book should be required reading for every pastor and every associate in the Body of Christ. It should be used as a textbook in every Bible college and university.

If we will allow the character of Christ to develop within each of us and serve one another, we shall come into the unity of the faith, and of the knowledge of the Son of God, unto a perfect man, unto the measure of the stature of the fullness of Christ.

Happy Caldwell
Agape Church
Little Rock, Arkansas

1
Revelation of an Armorbearer

One evening back in 1983, I felt a prompting to get alone with the Lord. I went into our living room and began to pray. Suddenly I was quickened in my spirit to read the story of David and Saul. I knew the Lord was ready to reveal something to me.

As I began to read, I came to 1 Samuel 16:21:

> **And David came to Saul, and stood before him: and he loved him greatly; and he became his armourbearer.**

Suddenly the Lord quickened the word *armourbearer* to me. He said, "I have called you to be Pastor Caldwell's *armorbearer.*"

What does an armorbearer do? In Old Testament days, he was the one responsible for carrying his master's shield into battle. He had the awesome responsibility of seeing to the safety of his officer.

God was getting my priorities in order at that time of my life. It is my prayer that, as you read this book, He will do the same for you.

The Spirit of an Armorbearer

We live in a world that seems to know very little about laying down one's life for another. A full understanding of this concept is vital to the Christian,

11

especially if he knows he has been called into the ministry.

Instead of offering ourselves to wait on others, we in the Church often expect them to wait on us. This is particularly true of our attitude toward the man or woman of God.

You and I will never flow in the anointing of Elisha until we have learned to serve an Elijah. Jesus said, **Greater love hath no man than this, that a man lay down his life for his friends** (John 15:13). It is not difficult to claim that we are submitted to Jesus, but the question is: are we submitted to another human being? That is a different story.

One day I asked God, "What about *my* dreams and desires?" He told me to give them to Him and to work at fulfilling the desires and visions of my pastor, assuring me that if I would do so, He would see to it that my dreams and desires would be fulfilled. He reminded me that that is exactly what Jesus did. He gave up His own will and desire in order to do the Father's will for His life. In turn, the Father made sure that Jesus' dreams and visions were all fulfilled.

The purpose of this book is to give you a revelation of *the spirit of an armorbearer* in your relationship with the man or woman of God in your life.

The Need for Armorbearers

My pastor understands the calling and anointing on my life, and it is his desire to see that calling fulfilled. On the other hand, I understand my God-given duty to stand with my pastor and help him fulfill the vision

God has given both of us, and to fully submit myself to him.

There is a great fear today among many pastors that their associates are out to steal the sheep from them. As a result, there is little or no trust between the pastor and his assistant, no flow between the two of them. I believe God has someone prepared for every pastor (and others of the five-fold ministry), someone to stand with him in the ministry.

I see today great ministries which are built around one person. What will happen when he is gone? It is of no credit to a pastor, or any man of God, to know that when he leaves town the sheep cannot function. The sheep should have their eyes fixed on Jesus, not the pastor. And there should be capable men to run the ministry while the pastor is absent.

Where would we be today if Jesus had not put a portion of Himself into the twelve disciples? What would have happened if, on the day He ascended to the Father, there had been no one there to see Him go and then to take up His ministry on earth?

I ask every pastor and spiritual leader this vital question: If you were taken off the scene today, where would your ministry be tomorrow? Most would have to admit that it would suffer. Jesus' ministry increased and multiplied. That's because there were armorbearers standing with Him.

Definition of the Word *Armorbearer*

The word *armorbearer* is listed eighteen times in Strong's concordance. All of the references are from the Old Testament. Each of these listings is referenced by two numbers, indicating that the word was originally translated from *two* Hebrew words.

Before beginning a study of the actual scriptures in which this word appears, let's consider its original meaning, which must be firmly established if the true idea of the term is to be fully understood.

As we have noted, the *King James* word *armourbearer* was translated from two Hebrew words. The first is *nasa* or *nacah (naw-saw')*. This is a primary word meaning "to *lift.*" It has a great variety of applications, both figuratively and literally. Some of the more interesting applications are to: accept, advance, bear, bear up, carry away, cast, desire, furnish, further, give, help, hold up, lift, pardon, raise, regard, respect, stir up, yield.

The second Hebrew word is *keliy (kel-ee')*, which comes from the root word *kalah (kaw-law')*, meaning "to *end.*" Some of the applications of this root word are to: complete, consume, destroy utterly, be done, finish, fulfill, long, bring to pass, wholly reap, make clean riddance.

From these two Hebrew words, we can see the duty of the armorbearer was to stand beside his leader to assist him, to lift him up, and to protect him against any enemy that might attack him.

Developing the Spirit of an Armorbearer

My purpose in writing this book is not to boast of how humble I have become by serving my pastor, but to help put an end to division in the Body of Christ. Like everyone who reads this book, I too have to deal with the temptation to get into strife, to refuse to submit in some areas of life. But the Lord has given me grace and I have learned to call upon Him and to trust Him completely to direct my steps.

You too can be set free from rebellion, strife and contention when you develop the spirit of an armorbearer.

Even though this book is written from the viewpoint and position of an associate minister, please do not think that it does not relate to you. It will help anyone who is a part of the Body of Christ, anyone who desires to fulfill his or her God-given call. To the person in the five-fold ministry, I say this: You will never arrive at a place where you do not have to submit to anyone. The spirit of an armorbearer is the spirit of Christ. It is the heart of a servant.

Now let's take a look into the function of an armorbearer.

2

Function of an Armorbearer

As we look at the function of an armorbearer, I would like for you to allow the Holy Spirit to quicken your heart and reveal to you where you may have failed to flow with your spiritual leaders. Make a quality decision to rid yourself of any trace of rebellion, strife, contention, competitiveness and unforgiveness; determining to faithfully fulfill your rightful place in the Body of Christ.

The main function of one who is designated as an armorbearer is that of service; he is to help and assist another. Let's look at some of the different forms this service takes.

Duties of an Armorbearer

An armorbearer...

1. Must provide strength for his leader.

By his very presence, a true armorbearer will always display and produce an attitude of faith and peace.

If you are to be successful in service as an armorbearer to your pastor, he must sense the joy and victory which is an integral part of your lifestyle. That alone will minister to him. It is a great relief to the pastor to know that he does not have to carry his assistant physically, mentally and spiritually. Many times I have seen pastors drained physically and emotionally because their associate was always in need of something. Your pastor has plenty of sheep to take care of; he doesn't need another. You should be assisting him, giving him much-needed rest in mind and body by demonstrating that your faith is strong and active.

2. Must have a deep-down sense of respect for his leader, and acceptance for, and tolerance of, his leader's personality and his way of doing things.

God made us all different. At least fifty percent of the time, your pastor's way of doing things will differ from yours. That difference should not be allowed to cause a problem for you or your spiritual leader.

Several years ago, I learned a secret which has helped me to flow in harmony with my pastor. I determined that if the end result of my pastor's plan is to build and extend the Kingdom of God and win souls for Jesus, then I am willing to flow with the plan. Our goal is the same, our methods different. But what does it really matter whose methods are used, as long as the goal is reached?

If you will adopt this attitude toward your pastor, there will be a knitting of hearts between the two of you. He will know that you are not there to argue with him or to challenge his decisions, but that you are there to work with him in achieving his God-given objectives.

3. Must instinctively understand his leader's thoughts.

I can hear what you are probably thinking right now: "My pastor and I just don't think alike." That's right; no two people do. And that is one of the problems which must be dealt with in being an armorbearer to another.

Instead of complaining about your differences, begin to discover and confess your agreement: "In Jesus' name, I understand how my pastor thinks and I flow with him in the spirit of understanding."

Remember, the disciples were with Jesus for three long years and yet they did not begin to think as He thought until after He had died, been buried and resurrected, ascended into heaven and sent the Holy Ghost. Just as God's Spirit was eventually imparted to these men, after a period of time your pastor's spirit will come upon you, and you two will become like-minded.

4. Must walk in agreement with and submission to his leader.

In order to be an armorbearer, you must have it settled in your heart that according to Romans 13:1,2, all authority is ordained of God. You must make up your mind to submit to your pastor in the same way that you would submit to Jesus.

Most Christians do not understand the true meaning of submission to authority. The Bible teaches that all authority has been instituted by God Himself, so to refuse to submit to God's delegated authority is to refuse to submit to God.

"Oh, but I will always submit myself to God!"

This is a comment I hear quite often. But how can a person claim to be submitted to God if he or she refuses to submit to God's delegated authority?

We must not look at the person, but at the office he occupies. We do not regard the man, but the position. We obey, not the individual himself, but God's authority in him. Anything less than full submission is rebellion, and rebellion is the principle on which Satan and his kingdom operate.

It is sad to think that we Christians can preach the truth with our lips, but go right on living by a satanic principle in our everyday lives. How can we expect to preach the Gospel to others and to bring them under God's authority if we ourselves have not yet fully submitted to that authority?

There is a spirit of independence at large in the Body of Christ today. Independent churches produce independent spirits. We must break this spirit and begin to rightly discern the whole Body of Christ.

The Apostle Peter tells us: **Likewise, ye younger, submit yourselves unto the elders...**(1 Pet. 5:5). There are no conditions to this command, except in the case of an elder who is giving directives which are in direct violation of the scriptures. Then the individual believer must obey a higher authority, which is God's Word.

Always remember this: God will never establish you as an authority until you have first learned to submit to authority.

5. Must make the advancement of his leader his most important goal.

When I asked the Lord, "What about *my* dreams and goals, the vision You have placed in *my* heart?" He said to me: "Son, you are not to live for the fulfillment of your dreams or vision. Set it as your goal to achieve your pastor's dreams, and I will make sure that yours are fulfilled."

I can honestly say that God has done that very thing in my life. Twelve years ago I had a vision to reach out into many nations. In 1982, I began to see that vision come to pass. I have already traveled to over twenty countries, and have preached in most of them. We are now establishing churches and Bible schools in five of those nations. All this has come about because I decided to do what Jesus did; He sacrificed His own desires in order to fulfill the Father's will. If you will do the same thing, God will exalt you, no matter what circumstances you may face.

6. Must possess endless strength so as to thrust, press and force his way onward without giving way under harsh treatment.

> **For what glory is it, if, when ye be buffeted for your faults, ye shall take it patiently? but if, when ye do well, and suffer for it, ye take it patiently, this is acceptable with God.**
>
> **1 Peter 2:20**

This passage makes it very clear that there will be times in the midst of battle when you and I will feel that we are being wrongfully treated. These types of situations are bound to arise, but do not allow Satan to put resentment into your heart. Learn to give the situation over to the Lord and endure what comes patiently; God will be pleased with you.

It may be that in your heart you know you made the right decision. But in the eyes of your leader, it may seem wrong. Such times will develop character in you, if you will walk in love, allowing the Spirit of God to take charge of the matter. Your strength will always come by encouraging yourself in the Lord, as David did in 1 Samuel 30:6.

The easy thing to do is quit, saying, "Well, no one around here appreciates me; I was rebuked and I know I was right in what I did." Do not give into the flesh.

Get in prayer and stay there until 1 Peter 2:20 has become a part of your very being. Victory will spring forth and you will say with David of old, "I will bless the Lord at all times." (Ps. 34:1.)

7. Must follow orders immediately and correctly.

In order to be a good leader, one must be a good follower. And being a good follower means taking care of things quickly and efficiently. If you aspire to become a leader, then the one you serve today must be able to depend upon you to carry out his directives. Here are some simple keys to help you to become a better follower so that some day you may be a better leader:

First, write everything down. I know what you're probably thinking: "Boy, what a revelation!" But let's be practical. God had everything written down for us so we would not forget anything. We dare not do any less for ourselves. Write down the orders of your leader just as a waiter writes down an order for food. Make sure your leader gets exactly *what he ordered.*

Second, ask your leader to explain anything you don't understand. Make sure you have the correct information before you leave to carry out the order. Many times we misrepresent our leader because we misunderstand what he means.

Third, treat your orders as highest priority. When asked to do something, do it immediately! I am always blessed when my secretary is efficient. Her efficiency ministers to me. The same results will come when you put your heart into carrying out instructions quickly and correctly.

8. Must be a support to his leader.

Every pastor needs a group of faithful supporters, especially among his associates and staff. The word supporter means "that which supports or upholds; a sustainer; a comforter; a maintainer; a defender."

Contrary to popular belief, pastors are human just like anyone else. They hurt; they make mistakes; they get frustrated and bothered; many times they face discouragement and disappointment. As armorbearers, our job is to uphold, sustain, maintain and defend our leader, being there for him to lean on in times of need.

Right now, as I am writing this, I am laughing because I can just hear the voice of some staff member or associate crying out: "What about *me?* What about *my* hurts, wounds and problems?" I will be honest with you. We have too many babies in the Body of Christ. It's time we started laying down our lives for someone else, putting our trust in God to take care of our hurts and frustrations.

There are many associates whose only desire and goal is to stand up in front of people and preach. They want to be in front of the pastor — until war breaks out; then they suddenly jump behind him! God has called you and me to go out in front of our pastor for only one reason, and that is to raise up our shield of faith and protect him from the harmful words of people and the fiery darts of the devil.

You will never make any real progress toward leadership until you have first mastered the art of supporting your spiritual leader.

9. *Must be an excellent communicator.*

Communication is more important than anything I know of in establishing a relationship with a leader.

It is the only way to build trust between the pastor and his associates. This does not mean that you are to bother your pastor with every issue or decision that comes up; just that you should let him be aware of what is going on in the church and among the people.

In my years of service as an associate minister, I have learned a very valuable lesson: *Never hide anything from your pastor.* Always let him know if someone is having (or causing) a problem in the church, and what steps you are taking to resolve that situation.

Many times I have to deal with things which I know are clearly in my area of responsibility, but I always make my pastor aware of what I am doing. Situations will sometimes arise which I know should be dealt with by the pastor himself. When that happens, I go and share with him. Either he will deal with the situation, or he will give me advice as to how to handle it.

The "bottom line" is communication.

If anyone ever says to you, "I want to tell you something in private, but you must promise not to let the pastor know I told you about it," you should stop that conversation immediately and say to the person, "You may as well hold your breath, because I will not make any such promise."

You owe it to your leader to reveal anything that is going to cause problems in the church. Jesus said that there is nothing hidden that will not be revealed. (Mark 4:22.) If you withhold something from your pastor, then I can safely prophesy that it will come back to you; it will blow up and you will be caught in the middle of the explosion.

Secrecy is a trap which Satan lays for the unsuspecting. Don't fall into it.

10. Must have a disposition that will eagerly gain victories for his leader.

In 2 Samuel 22:36 David said of the Lord, **...thy gentleness hath made me great.** David was a great warrior, but he declared that it wasn't his boldness, assurance or strength that made him great; rather, it was God's gentleness. This is the character trait that will gain victories for the leader and the one who serves him as armorbearer.

Armed with this attitude, you will represent your leader well and gain much favor. Always remember that as an associate or assistant, wherever you go and whatever you do, you represent your pastor. You do not want to do anything to bring a reproach to him or the church you both serve.

I have seen times when the pastor has asked an associate to make some changes throughout his department. The associate then calls his staff together and tells them: "Pastor has said that you had better straighten up or out you go." That makes a pastor look as if he is some kind of unholy, ruthless king sitting on his throne barking out orders.

This kind of thing happens all the time in churches, and the result is always strife. The only reason any associate would say such a thing is to make it look as if he really cares for the people under him, but the pastor doesn't. It is just an attempt to save his own reputation at the expense of the pastor's. A true armorbearer will always strive to represent his pastor well before all men.

When we work with people, we face many delicate situations every day. Even though you are not the shepherd of the flock, as an associate you must take into your spirit the heart of a shepherd. You must learn to deal with people in love and find some common ground of agreement with the ones with whom you work and deal. No one is unreachable as long as he is teachable.

In my fifteen years of experience as an associate, I have sat with people and explained to them what my pastor meant by a statement he has made. Some people are easily offended, and many times they will come to the associate before going directly to the pastor. When people come to me in such situations, I try to help them understand what my pastor really meant because I know his heart. From there, I encourage them to make an appointment to meet with him personally to discuss the matter.

I encourage you to trust God every day for a spirit of *humility, meekness, forgiveness, purity* and a *clear conscience.* These virtues will keep a guard around you, and then what an asset you will be to the ministry.

11. Must have the ability to minister strength and courage to his leader.

In order to minister strength and courage, an armorbearer must possess an endless fountain of these virtues himself. The word *courage* means "bravery; the ability to encounter difficulties and danger with firmness, boldness and valor."

When your pastor stands up and says, "Thus saith the Lord, 'Build the church building without going into debt,' " what is your reaction?

Some may say, "The pastor is really missing it this time."

How do you respond?

Remember when the children of Israel were told to go into the Promised Land and overcome it? (Numbers 13.) They sent twelve spies into the land who came back and reported on what they had seen there. Only two of the twelve had the courage to say, "Let's go up and take it, for we are well able to do so." (v. 30.) Everyone else said, "No, we can't do it."

Whenever God speaks to your Moses, then be like Joshua and Caleb, the two strong, courageous spies. Stand up in faith and courage and go forth to take the land — no matter how big the task may be.

In Numbers 14:4 we read this about the faithless, fearful children of Israel: **And they said one to another, Let us make a captain, and let us return into Egypt.** Many times the first choice of a new captain will be the associate minister. When a portion of the people begin to call out for you to become their new leader — beware. When they are ready to make you captain in place of the pastor, because you will lead them the way they want to go — look out! That is a deception and temptation from Satan. That is not the way to success and life, it is the way into sin and rebellion. God is never in such a movement.

Courage comes from faith in God. In order to minister the same assurance your pastor has, you must stay built up in the Word of God. This edification comes only by putting the Word first.

Another deception and temptation from Satan which must be guarded against and overcome is the false idea that the pastor is more concerned with fulfilling his own personal vision than he is with meeting the needs of his associates and staff members. The lie is that the pastor will go to any limits to accomplish his own goal, but will not go out of his way to help meet the goals of those who work with him.

Remember one thing: the vision of the church you are called to serve is God's vision, and if He did not think you could fit in with it, He would never have placed you in that ministry to begin with. You will not always get a pat on the back for doing a good job. As Christians, our rewards are waiting for us in heaven. Would you prefer for your pastor to pat you on the back and say, "Good job," or for Jesus to pat you on the back and say, "Well done, good and faithful servant"?

God is a wonderful accountant, and some day the books will be opened and the rewards distributed. I trust that your rewards will be great. They will be determined by your attitude here and now on this earth.

Functions of an Armorbearer

Now let's look at some other functions of the armorbearer in order to get a better understanding of the loyalty and the attitude of heart which must be developed to fulfill this divine calling.

The true armorbearer:

_____ Awakens and arouses his leader, helping him to stand against all foes.

_____ Carries and handles his leader's weapons resourcefully.

_____ Moves quickly alongside his leader through the thick of battle as a forceful escort who never falls behind.

_____ Protects and watches out for his leader continually and continuously.

_____ Repels any type of attack against his leader.

_____ Rescues his leader from all difficulties and hardships.

_____ Moves to resist totally and completely every enemy advance which comes against his leader to do him harm.

_____ Opposes and routs his leader's enemies swiftly and forcefully.

_____ Remains always on duty at his leader's side to tend to any need which may arise.

_____ Keeps one eye on the leader at all times and the other eye trained on the enemy, anticipating the actions of both.

_____ Surrenders completely to his leader, trusting him implicitly and obeying without hesitation his every command.

_____ Carries out every plan of his leader successfully.

_____ Completes his leader's commands perfectly.

_____ Assists his leader in all activities and undertakings.

_____ Organizes and arranges his leader's activities.

_____ Prepares and cares for his leader's belongings.

_____ Takes very special care in the selection and preparation of his leader's supplies.

_____ Anticipates his leader's needs and demands so as to properly furnish and supply what is needed.

_____ Keeps his eye on the road ahead so as to point out to his leader any danger or pitfall.

_____ Recognizes and brings to his leader's attention any questionable matters or any vital information.

_____ Strives to make his leader's surroundings more pleasant and bearable.

_____ Develops an eye for detail.

_____ Helps bring an acceleration in growth and promotion to his leader's progress.

_____ Places primary emphasis on enhancing the leader's position, guarding against any personal jealousy, envy or selfishness.

_____ Exalts, respects and uplifts his leader at all times.

_____ Watches for his officer's every reward, claiming those which the leader may have overlooked.

_____ Works tirelessly and diligently on behalf of his leader, seeking ways to advance his welfare and situation.

_____ Fulfills his leader in every way, getting along with him, and making him feel comfortable in giving orders.

_____ Sacrifices his own life and well-being for the betterment of his leader.

_____ Works for his leader's welfare at all time.

_____ Demonstrates total intolerance of any false charge made against his leader.

_____ Shares the dreams, goals and visions of his leader.

_____ Desires to see his leader "get ahead."

_____ Forgives his leader for any offense immediately and without harboring resentment or anger.

_____ Refuses to hold a grudge against his leader for any reason.

_____Demonstrates extreme loyalty to his leader, even unto death.

_____ Completes and complements his leader.

_____ Flows well with his leader.

_____ Esteems his leader as more important than himself.

It is obvious by now that a biblical armorbearer was much more than just a hired hand. An armorbearer was a person who undoubtedly spent many years, if not his entire life, in his officer's service. Only in this manner could he come to know and understand his officer.

Servant, bodyguard, friend, companion, butler, cook and confidant are just some of the many roles the armorbearer filled in the life of his officer. His list of duties was interminable. The position of armorbearer is one which requires great honor, love, tolerance and watchfulness. Unquestioning obedience was absolutely necessary, although after a few years of service the faithful armorbearer probably did not need to be told what his officer thought, desired or required. He knew him as he knew himself.

Dedication and devotion unto death was the order of each day for the biblical armorbearer.

Although there is no reference material available to indicate the exact procedure involved in the selection and training of an armorbearer in biblical days, it seems clear that whatever method was used, it was obviously a position of heartfelt loyalty. It is also evident that the armorbearer was chosen and trained by the officer he would serve.

In Chapter 5 we will consider some of the qualifications for this vital position of spiritual armorbearer.

3

Armorbearers of the Old Testament

A good example of the loyalty of an armorbearer is found in the story of the death of Abimelech. (Judges 9:45-55.)

This event took place during a war in which Abimelech was laying siege to a city. He was succeeding in his attempt to seize the city and had the enemy on the run. When he came to a tower where many of the people had taken refuge, he was prepared to burn it down. As wood was being laid at the foot of the tower, a woman in the top threw down a piece of millstone which struck Abimelech on the head, cracking his skull. He went to his armorbearer and ordered the young man, **...Draw thy sword, and slay me, that men say not of me, A woman slew him...**(v. 54).

Even though Abimelech was wicked, the loyalty of his armorbearer is obvious. He was the closest person to the king when the stone struck him on the head. He was just as concerned about Abimelech's tainted honor as Abimelech was himself. He did not want it said that his officer had been killed by a woman. His instant obedience is also recorded: **...And his young man thrust him through, and he died** (v. 54).

Saul's Armorbearer

In 1 Samuel 31:4-6 and 1 Chronicles 10:4,5, we find another account of an officer at war, his armorbearer at his side. Saul and his army were fighting against the Philistines and were losing ground. Saul's army, realizing that defeat was imminent, turned to flee. His men, including his sons, were killed and Saul was wounded by arrows. He turned to his armorbearer and ordered him: ...**Draw thy sword, and thrust me though therewith; lest these uncircumcised come and thrust me through, and abuse me...**(1 Sam. 31:4).

Saul wanted to die at the hands of his armorbearer rather than be captured and tortured by the enemy. However, his armorbearer would not oblige him, so Saul took his own life by falling on his sword. **And when his armourbearer saw that Saul was dead, he fell likewise upon his sword, and died with him** (v. 5).

There are many things revealed in this portion of scripture.

At some point in the battle, Saul's forces turned to flee. His army was put to rout, his men killed. Later on in the chase, his three sons were slain. The enemy came close enough to wound Saul. That was when he turned to his armorbearer and made his request to die at his hands.

Note that although everyone else had fled, leaving Saul to face the whole enemy army alone, his faithful armorbearer was right alongside of him. Saul, being the king, rode on the back of the fastest horse or in the swiftest chariot. If he traveled by chariot, then his armorbearer was his driver. If he went on horseback, then Saul's horse must have been chosen by his armorbearer because it was part of his duty to select and care for his officer's mount, equipment and supplies. Needless to say, the armorbearer's horse had to be of equal strength, speed and stamina as his master's.

The armorbearer could be trusted to choose and select for his officer because he knew how his commander thought and what he liked and needed.

Through all the fighting and fleeing, Saul's armorbearer had managed to dodge the arrows and stay right alongside his leader. When Saul commanded his faithful servant to thrust him through with his sword, **...his armourbearer would not; for he was sore afraid...**(v. 4).

It seems peculiar that an armorbearer would be "sore afraid." He had been selected, trained and prepared to serve in battle. Because he was an armorbearer to the king, he was probably more skilled in warfare than any other soldier in the king's army. His duty was to protect the commander-in-chief. It doesn't seem logical that a man who was trained and prepared to give his life to save and defend the king would be afraid.

In the Hebrew, this word translated afraid in the *King James Version* is *yare' (yaw-ray')*. It does not mean to fear in the sense of being frightened or terrorized, but to fear out of *reverence!* In this case, it means "to *sorely respect and honor"!*

Now the armorbearer's reaction is much more understandable.

This man had spent all his time in Saul's service, caring for and protecting him. His entire reason for being was the preservation of the life of the king. If there was even the slightest chance that Saul could be saved from destruction, then he had to take that chance, regardless of the odds against its success.

Perhaps it was just too much to ask the man who had protected Saul all this time to take the very life he was pledged to defend. He just could not bring himself to destroy the one he had spent his life preserving and protecting.

Two Different Armorbearers

Notice the reaction of Saul's armorbearer as contrasted with that of Abimelech's servant, who did kill his officer when ordered to do so. Here we see two different reactions from men both of whom had dedicated and sacrificed their lives to the welfare of their superiors. Perhaps the reason their reactions were different is because the circumstances were different.

Although Saul had been severely wounded by arrows, perhaps his armorbearer did not judge his wounds to be fatal. The young man was probably trained in attending to battle wounds. Perhaps he would have preferred to try to outrun the Philistines and hide somewhere, so he could nurse Saul back to health.

Abimelech had been hit on the head with a large piece of millstone, and his skull had been crushed. The wound was probably not very pretty. Perhaps the contents of his skull were coming out of the wound. Death seemed inevitable.

Saul said, "Draw your sword and thrust me through, lest these uncircumcised come and thrust me through and abuse me."

Abimelech said, "Draw your sword and kill me, so people won't say that I was killed by a woman."

The difference is that Abimelech was dying; Saul was not. Saul simply feared that the Philistines would come and torture him.

Perhaps Saul's armorbearer would rather have tried to escape with his commander, or maybe even to fight to the death alongside him. But one thing is for sure: out of *respect*, he could not be the one to put an end to Saul's life. It was a sense of reverential fear, respect and honor, not "fright" that caused the armorbearer to fail to obey his king.

When Saul realized that his armorbearer would not comply with his request, he fell on his own sword. In true armorbearer fashion, as a man who had spent his whole life following Saul, the armorbearer knew that this was no time to stop now. When his master fell on his own sword and ended his life, the armorbearer had no more reason to live. Out of respect for his officer, he also fell on his sword. Suicide had not been his idea. In fact, if Saul had asked, his armorbearer may have even had a better strategy or a plan to escape from the hands of the Philistines. But since Saul chose to end his life, so did his faithful servant.

Jonathan's Armorbearer

In 1 Samuel 14:1-23 there is another account of a relationship between a young man and his armorbearer. Jonathan ordered his armorbearer to accompany him over to the garrison of the Philistines against whom he and the other Israelites were warring. He wanted to go over single-handed. Jonathan had not told his father, Saul, of his intentions. Though the king knew nothing about the plan, and though he and his master were only two against an entire army, Jonathan's armorbearer obeyed.

In verse 6, Jonathan says: **...Come, and let us go over unto the garrison of these uncircumcised: it may be that the Lord will work for us: for there is no restraint to the Lord to save by many or by few.** In verse 7, the young and fearless armorbearer answers: **...Do all that is in thine heart: turn thee; behold, I am with thee according to thy heart.**

As the two young men climbed up toward the enemy's camp, God confirmed to them that He had, in fact, delivered the enemy into their hand. Jonathan turned to his companion and said, **...Come up after me...**(v. 12).

When they reached the place where the enemy was standing, **....they fell before Jonathan; and his armourbearer slew after him** (v. 13.) Then the passage goes on to explain how God saved the whole nation of Israel that day, through the brave actions of Jonathan and his faithful, obedient armorbearer.

It is curious to note that Jonathan said, "It *may* be that the Lord will work for us." Although Jonathan was not certain about what would happen, his armorbearer was more than willing to follow. Verse 7 reveals his answer, and the proper attitude of any armorbearer:

> ..."Do all that is in your heart. Go then; here I am with you, according to your heart."
> **New King James Version**

> ...Do all that is in your mind; I am with you in whatever you think [best].
> **The Amplified Bible**

> "Do all that you have in mind....Go ahead; I am with you heart and soul."
>
> **New International Version**
>
> ..."Whatever you want to do, I am with you."
>
> **Good News Version**
>
> "Fine!....Do as you think best; I'm with you heart and soul, whatever you decide."
>
> **The Living Bible**

As they approached the enemy, Jonathan's armorbearer knew his place. He was to come *after* Jonathan.

In verse 13 we see that it was the anointing upon Jonathan, the anointing of a leader, that caused the enemy to fall. The young armorbearer was diligent to follow along *after* his officer, destroying the enemy who had been knocked to the ground by God's anointing upon his leader: ". . .and his armourbearer slew after him." (v. 13.)

This is a classic example of the humility and diligence of a biblical armorbearer. He is one who wins victories and slays enemies while his leader gets the glory...one who trusts his officer, even in what may appear to be a whim...one who takes his place *behind* the man he serves, not striving to get out in front.

David as Armorbearer

In 1 Samuel 16:14-23 we find the story of the last of the five armorbearers.

King Saul was troubled. He had a distressing spirit. He decided to find a skillful musician who could ease his state of mind when he was oppressed. A young man was recommended to the king by one of his servants:

> ...Behold, I have seen a son of Jesse the Bethlehemite, that is cunning in playing, and a mighty valiant man, and a man of war, and prudent in matters, and a comely person, and the Lord is with him.
>
> 1 Samuel 16:18

The young man was sent to Saul, bearing gifts. We are told that Saul "loved him greatly" and made him his armorbearer. (v. 21.) He could minister strength to Saul, causing him to feel "refreshed" and "well." (v. 23.)

In verse 18 we see that the young armorbearer was described as:

1. Skillful in playing
2. A mighty man of valor
3. A man of war
4. Prudent in speech
5. Handsome in appearance
6. One whom the Lord was with

All of these qualities are biblical descriptions of a true armorbearer.

Perhaps the fact that David had once been Saul's armorbearer further explains his attitude when he later declared that he would not touch "the Lord's anointed." (1 Sam. 26:9.) No matter how hard Saul tried to kill David, and no matter how many opportunities David had to slay Saul, David never struck back.

Did David walk in the same fear that caused Saul's future armorbearer to refuse to kill him? More than likely. This respect and honor toward God's anointed may also explain David's attitude of extreme repentance, sorrow and humility before Saul after he had sneaked up behind the king in a cave and cut off the edge of his robe. (1 Sam. 24:1-6.)

David was a true armorbearer, one who held no grudges but who faithfully and obediently withstood his captain's harsh treatment. The result was his own eventual promotion to a place of high respect and honor.

4

New Testament Armorbearing

Thus far we have investigated the Old Testament concerning the subject of armorbearing, and we have clearly defined the duty, role and service of the armorbearer in his Old Testament function. Now let's look more closely at this role of armorbearing in the light of the New Testament.

The Ministry of Armorbearing

In the life of every Christian, God has established a certain order of priorities. Both the armorbearer and the person he is serving should follow these priorities, if they are to live faithful Christian lives. In descending order of importance, these priorities are:

1. Relationship with God
2. Relationship with spouse
3. Relationship with children
4. Employment or work

One of the main differences between armorbearing in the Old Testament and in the New Testament is the fact that in Old Testament days the duty of an armorbearer was priority number one. In the New Testament, armorbearing is priority number four. This doesn't mean that today's armorbearer is to take less than necessary care of his responsibility. His position is a God-given one, and he must be a good steward of that duty. Although the physical roles may have changed, the attitude of the heart must be the same.

The position of armorbearer is not likely to be one to which God would call a person for only a short period of time; rather, it remains a position of devotion and heartfelt loyalty.

In comparing this office to the office of an associate or any position of the ministry, the individual must realize that God has not called him to use that position as a stepping stone. We have seen this happen so many times in the Body of Christ, and it is a reproach to God.

If a person feels that the only reason God has him where he is now is so he can be promoted to "something bigger and better," then it's sad to say but that individual is operating in the world's system. This type of individual says, "Whoever offers me the most money or authority gets my services."

Did you ever stop and ask God if your current position is the one He has chosen for you, if where you are now is where He wants you to be? It makes no difference what the salary or working conditions are like; what really matters is, has God called you to that job and place?

While serving my pastor, I have had two opportunities to become the pastor of another church. Both of these were good churches, and at the time of the offers the pay would have been better than what I was receiving where I am. Besides all that, I could have been the pastor, rather than an associate. If I had operated by the world's system, I would have jumped at the "chance for advancement." But the Kingdom of God does not operate that way.

I know that I am in God's *divinely appointed* position for me. That is how I pray for the people who come to join the staff in our church. I say, "Lord, send us the people who are divinely appointed by You to be here and work with us."

Unless your people are divinely *called* and *sent* to you by the Lord, you do not want them. I understand that there will be times when God will separate a person from his current position. That moment may come for you one day. But if it does come, you and your pastor will know in the spirit that it is time for a change, and that the separation will be best for all concerned, expecially the Kingdom of God.

On my office wall there hangs a plaque which reads: "Bloom where you are planted." I believe and practice that principle, which is based on God's Word. My life is a testimony that the Word of God works.

As armorbearers we must prove ourselves faithful where God has "planted" us. Let God exalt and promote you where you are. If you will be diligent, faithful, humble and motivated by the heart of a servant, you will find the principles of God's Word working for you.

The Bible tells us, "Humble yourself before God, and He will exalt you." (1 Pet. 5:6.) I know in my heart that if God ever says it's time for me to leave this position and move on to another, the pastor and I will both know it.

Faithful Armorbearing

I would like to share an interesting story with you as an illustration of faithful armorbearing. Some time ago my pastor, Happy Caldwell of Agape Church in Little Rock, Arkansas, met with the Billy Graham Crusade team which was planning a series of meetings in our city. The crusade coordinator began his talk by stating that he had been with Billy Graham the least amount of time of any of the ministers on the staff.

"I have only been with Billy for 23 *years*," he said.

When I heard that, I was shocked. In charismatic circles we preach faithfulness and staying with something, but the Billy Graham Crusade team lives it. Some staff members and ministers are ready to give up and go on to their reward if God doesn't open up something new and better for them every year. We have got to start seeing our position as one called and instituted of God. We must be willing to stay in it for the rest of our lives, if that is what God wants.

Recently I got on my face before God and prayed, "Lord, if it is Your desire that I stay here as my pastor's armorbearer and serve this ministry in that capacity for the rest of my life, then Your will be done."

Friend, it is no fun to be out of the will of God. We in the Church no longer have the time to be operating outside of the will and plan of our heavenly Father.

If you are an associate or staff minister, I want to encourage you to remain faithful, no matter what pressure you may be facing. I will honestly admit that there have been times when I have wanted to throw in the towel and say to God, "This is too hard; this is not fair."

One day Jesus spoke to me and told me that He was simply asking me to do the same thing He had done on the earth. Jesus fulfilled His Father's desire, and not His own. He is not asking you and me to do anything He Himself has not already done.

At this moment in my life, I am doing more than I have ever done for God. At thirty-three years of age, I travel overseas and do things that I have always dreamed of. I believe it is because I have stayed where God put me.

One day a man came into my office, which is really nice with a beautiful view of a small mountain right behind my desk.

"Well," he said, as he walked in, "how does it feel to be a big man with a huge desk, leather chairs and a view like you've got there?"

Thank the Lord I was in a good mood when he said that. People have no idea what it has taken to get to that place. Any staff minister can relate to my feelings.

If you are not a staff member, I will tell you how it feels. It feels exactly the same way it felt in 1979 when I had an office with a pea-green carpet, an army surplus desk and a small window with a view of the back of a drug store. Did I complain? Heavens, no! Pastor Caldwell had a door laid over two small filing cabinets for a desk. I was jumping up and down with excitement just to be able to say to someone, "Come into my office." It was ugly, but it was *my* office, the first real one I had ever had. I had "birthed" it in the spirit in prayer, and I was as happy and proud of it as I could be.

The Spirit of God may be ministering to you right now because you are at the place of giving up in your ministry. Please don't! Get in the Word and start rejoicing in what you have been blessed with. Put your future into God's hands. Remember, David was faithful to Saul, and look how God exalted him.

One day I walked into my office with everything in the world coming against me. I was discouraged. I felt left out. It seemed that God was going to just have to move me on. At that time, I looked at the Bible on my desk and I cried out to God, saying, "I need help!" I picked up the Bible and it fell open to Ephesians 5. I know God divinely directed me to that chapter. I began to read, and then I came to Ephesians 5:17-19:

> ...be ye not unwise, but understanding what the will of the Lord is.
>
> And be not drunk with wine, wherein is excess; but be filled with the Spirit;
>
> Speaking to yourselves in psalms and hymns and spiritual songs, singing and *making* melody in your heart to the Lord.

As I read that passage, the Lord quickened the word *making* to me. "Son," He said, "a piano makes beautiful music only when someone sits down and plays it."

"The joy, peace, and assurance you need is there," He went on to say, "but you have to make the melody come forth. Get up and start dancing before Me."

I did not want to do that, nor did I feel like it, but I did it in faith. I closed my office door and started to leap and jump for joy, praising God. As I did so, the anointing broke the yoke of oppression.

If you are under a spirit of oppression, then before you read any further in this chapter, get up and start rejoicing. You are set free in Jesus' name. This is God's will for you right now.

Now what about our personal relationship with our officer? In 2 Corinthians 5:16 the Apostle Paul says: **Wherefore, henceforth know we no man after the flesh....** As an armorbearer, you have a called ministry to serve a general of God's army. The Old Testament suggests a very close physical relationship between the officer and his armorbearer. This may be the case in the New Testament, but such a close personal relationship is not necessary to successfully carry out the responsibility of the armorbearer. God did not call you to be your leader's fishing buddy. I am not called to be my pastor's best friend. We are friends, but that is not our primary relationship.

We should never assume a personal right to know or be a part of our officer's family or private life:

> **Be not forward [self-assertive and boastfully ambitious] in the presence of the king, and stand not in the place of great men;**
>
> **For better it is that it be said to you, Come up here, than that you should be put lower in the presence of the prince whose eyes have seen you.**
> **Proverbs 25:6,7 AMP**

I will say this, that a personal relationship of some kind is inevitable, but the armorbearer's primary role is not that of personal friend. The armorbearer's main purpose is to pull down Satan's strongholds for his pastor, church and city. Do not get your feelings hurt if you are not asked to have dinner with the pastor every Friday night. Your goal is not to get next to the pastor, but to get next to Jesus and to do battle in the Spirit.

The Service of an Armorbearer

In the Old Testament, the armorbearer's main function was directly related to combat. This has not changed at all between the Old and New Testaments. What has changed greatly is the type of combat in which the New Testament armorbearer is to engage as he serves his officer:

> **For we wrestle not against flesh and blood, but against principalities, against powers, against the rulers of the darkness of this world, against spiritual wickedness in high places.**
>
> **Ephesians 6:12**

In this passage we clearly see that we are not engaged in battle against the Philistines — against flesh and blood — but against demonic powers.

God calls men and women to do great things and to accomplish wondrous tasks for Him. Preaching the Word of God to all nations is no small undertaking. It is impossible for one person to accomplish it alone. That's where the Body of Christ comes in. God will place *His* vision inside a person, and *His* anointing upon him to carry it forth. Then He will surround that individual with other people who will support and work with him toward the fulfillment of that vision. The Lord will begin by sending God-called ministers to assist the man of God and to take his spirit upon them. These people act as armorbearers; their function is to take the load off their officer, and to help impart his vision to the people.

I have heard preachers refer to the associate ministry as "playing second fiddle." I have a few questions that I would like to ask those who think that way: Did Joshua play second fiddle to Moses? Did

Elisha play second fiddle to Elijah? Does a person's nose play second fiddle to his eyes? Does his foot play second fiddle to his hand?

If you have thought of the associate ministry in this way, I hope that by now your thinking has begun to change.

There is no second fiddle position in the Body of Christ.

> **And those members of the body, which we think to be less honourable, upon these we bestow more abundant honour; and our uncomely parts have more abundant comeliness.**
>
> **1 Corinthians 12:23**

If anyone thinks that because he fills the position of pastor, prophet, apostle, evangelist or teacher he is better than the rest of the Body, then he had better prepare to be brought low, for that is pride, and destruction is waiting for him right around the corner. I trust that you never fall for that kind of deceptive thinking.

God-called armorbearers are there to support the leader and to help fulfill the vision God has given him.

There came a day in my life when I told my pastor that I was behind him. He stopped and said, "No, you are standing with me."

That did not happen overnight, but no relationship is built overnight. Your position in the ministry is important to God, and if you are faithful and patient, you will be exalted in due season.

Deuteronomy 32:30 says that one shall put a thousand to flight, and two will chase ten thousand. See, with you by his side, your officer is ten times more powerful than he is alone.

The Duties of the Armorbearer

We can see that the most important part of the armorbearer's duties lie in the spirit realm. Armorbearing is a ministry of prayer, watchfulness, and intercession. The armorbearer is to prove his sincerity, loyalty, and courage in the spirit realm through prayer and intercession. All the physical tasks of an Old Testament armorbearer apply today, in the spirit. From what we have learned from the Old Testament, based on what we see in the New Testament scriptures, we are able to identify the duties of a New Testament armorbearer.

A true armorbearer:

_____ Strives to keep his godly priorities in line.

_____ Resists seeking to know his leader after the flesh.

_____ Remains always humble, with fear and trembling, in sincerity of heart, doing what is pleasing to Christ, "not with eyeservice as menpleasers."

_____ Serves his leader well, expecting no reward from man, but knowing that Jesus will reward him one day for his efforts and loyalty.

_____ Aids his leader in spiritual combat.

_____ Ministers strength to his leader in the spirit.

_____ Helps his leader to stand against the wiles of the devil.

_____ Knows how to deal with spiritual forces.

Even though the word *armorbearer* is not used in the New Testament, we can see from the scriptures that the attitude and spirit of an armorbearer is found throughout the pages of the New Covenant.

Here are some references to help you discover and study for yourself the proper attitude and character of a New Testament armorbearer: Matt. 18:1-4; John 15:13; Eph. 6:5,6; Phil. 2:3-9; 1 Thess. 5:12,13; 1 Pet. 5:5; 2:20.

5

The Cry of God's Leaders

"Oh, God! Send me a Joshua!"

Now we all know that Joshua was never referred to in the Bible as Moses' armorbearer, but was called Moses' minister in Joshua 1:1. The verb form of the word *minister* means: to attend, to contribute to, to minister to, to wait on, and to serve. From this definition we see that Joshua's duty was to wait on Moses, to contribute to his success, and to serve him in everything that he did. Had Moses had an armorbearer, it would have been Joshua because of their relationship.

Today apostles, prophets, evangelists, pastors and teachers all across our land are crying out for a man like Joshua to come to their aid. But my question to them is: Are you willing to be a Moses to your Joshua? Now that puts the shoe on the other foot.

What about you? Moses was willing to invest his anointing, and his whole life, into Joshua. He was willing to relinquish control and allow Joshua to take the people on into the Promised Land, even though Moses had personally shepherded the people for forty years in the wilderness. He knew that the children of Israel belonged to God, not to him. He obeyed God when the voice came saying, "Now Joshua will be the one to bring them into the land which I have promised to give them."

I am not saying that this is the situation in your ministry, but I would like for you to see, first of all, that *it's not your ministry,* it's God's.

God placed the vision in you. He birthed it in your spirit. When God starts something, He finishes it. The work God has begun will continue long after you — if you are willing to put yourself into other people, without fear of giving them the authority they need to help you. You can tell how good a leader is by the quality of people following after him.

Here is a list of the basic things to look for, and to do, when seeking a Joshua for your own ministry:

1. Pray for God's divinely-appointed people to come your way.

This is always priority number one.

Ask God to send you quality people to carry your vision forward. The people whom God sends you may be your own personal family, or they may not be.

I once heard a minister say, "I would never let anybody but a member of the family run my ministry." That's a very strong statement, and totally *unscriptural.* The unity between a leader and his staff is in the spirit and not by blood.

God raised up Joshua, not one of Moses' children. God raised up David and elected him to be king, and not Jonathan, who was legal heir to the throne. God told Elijah to go and anoint Elisha as his successor, not one of Elijah's own family members. God anointed Samuel to be priest, not the sons of Eli. In fact, Hophni and Phineas, Eli's sons, were full of evil and wickedness. (1 Sam. 2:22-25.)

Now I will say that God may raise up your son or daughter to carry on your vision, but He could send someone else. The key is for you to do the will of God for your ministry no matter who He may choose to help and succeed you.

Whatever kind of people you need, ask God for them. He will send you an associate, a music director, a head usher, or whatever you may need or desire. You just need to petition Him, and start thanking Him for answering your prayer.

2. Be willing to invest yourself in the lives of your helpers.

Some leaders wonder why they have problems with their staff. Many times the reason is because they have never invested themselves in their associates.

In the Old Testament, the Lord spoke to Moses about those who had been chosen to assist him in leading the children of Israel:

> **And I will come down and talk with thee there: and I will take of the spirit which is upon thee, and will put it upon them; and they shall bear the burden of the people with thee, that thou bear it not thyself alone.**
>
> **Numbers 11:17**

At this time God took the spirit that He had put upon Moses and placed it upon the seventy elders. This was for these elders to function and minister to the people with the same love and anointing with which Moses operated. This was accomplished when Moses laid his hands on his associates, thus imparting the spirit to them.

Where would we be today had Jesus not invested Himself in the disciples? What would have happened if His attitude had been, "I am the leader here, and I don't have time to waste on you weak, faithless disciples"? This kind of attitude has been evident in some leaders, and it is of the devil, not of God. The Lord has not called any of us to control the lives of other people, but to be an example to the flock.

3. Delegate authority.

God desires to send you quality people who can flow with you. But do not be afraid to let them fully express their God-given creativity. Sometimes leaders live in fear that they are losing control because others are beginning to grasp the vision and "run with it."

Do not stifle the enthusiasm, anointing, wisdom and ability of your staff. A smart leader knows how to direct the talents and abilities of his people. You must provide opportunities for your staff members to develop, minister and release their latent creativity. This applies especially to armorbearers who have proven themselves faithful to bless you and help you minister to the people.

If you are going to give anyone responsibility in any area, then be big enough to give him the authority he needs to carry out that responsibility.

An official from Washington, D.C., shared how he had a real problem with authority. He liked the feeling of power it gave him. After becoming a Christian and being called to the pastorate, he said that it was still a struggle for him to delegate authority. In order to break this spirit, he shared how he began to "sow" authority in others.

You will find that, with God, the more you give away, the more God will give back to you.

4. *Look for the spirit of an armorbearer in people.*

Here is a checklist for determining if the people who come your way have the qualifications to become armorbearers:

A. Do they have a disciplined prayer life?

B. Are they faithful to the church?

C. Is their family intact?

D. Are they tithers?

E. Are you at ease in their presence?

F. Are they at ease in your presence?

G. Are they interested in people of all types and races?

H. Do they possess a strong and steady will?

I. Do they avoid murmuring and complaining?

J. Are they optimistic?

K. Do they submit to authority?

L. Are they good listeners?

M. Are they disciplined mentally and physically?

N. Are they loyal?

As you ask and answer these questions about others, always remember to ask *yourself* this important question: *What good is a general without an army to follow him?*

6

How to Develop the Spirit of an Armorbearer

Every child of God, from leaders on down, needs to develop the character of an armorbearer. I believe that, right now in the Body of Christ, we need teaching on the development of the *character of Christ*. We have learned a lot about faith, prosperity and intercession, but I feel we have got to place more emphasis on character development. God's power is hindered because of our lust for power, money and sex. These things are currently destroying ministries around the world.

I would like to share some steps which I believe will be beneficial to follow in your effort to develop the spirit of a true God-called armorbearer.

Steps to the Development of the Spirit of an Armorbearer

Step 1. Free yourself from pride. (James 4:6.)

Evidences of pride are:

A. An independent spirit (refusal to look to God or others for help).

B. A failure to admit mistakes.

C. A lack of a teachable spirit.

D. A rebellious attitude toward those in authority.

E. A proud countenance.

F. Self-centered conversation.

G. Intolerance toward the mistakes of others.

H. A bossy attitude.

Step 2: Free yourself from anger. (Prov. 16:32.)

Evidences of anger are:

A. Temper tantrums (at any age).

B. An angry reaction to supposed injustice.

C. Expressed frustration over unchangeable circumstances.

D. Grumbling, murmuring and complaining.

E. Extreme sensitivity and touchiness.

Step 3: Free yourself from immorality. (2 Cor. 7:1.)

Evidences of a spirit of impurity are:

A. Sensual conversation.

B. The reading of impure materials.

C. An impure attitude and improper actions toward members of the opposite sex.

D. A desire to listen to sensual music.

E. Sensual dress or appearance.

F. Carnal curiosity.

Step 4: Free yourself from bitterness. (Heb. 12:15.)

Evidences of a spirit of bitterness are:

A. Sarcastic and critical talk.

B. An inability to trust people.

C. Frequent illness.

D. Self-pity.

E. A sad countenance.

These are all areas in which we need to judge ourselves in order to break Satan's power in our life, to be pleasing to God, and to be the light of the world. This will be accomplished as we lead a life above reproach, giving ourselves totally and freely one for another.

We are God's armorbearers. We are to carry the shield for one another, joining our faith together. If we will do that, we will truly become *God's Great Army.* We will go forth to conquer in the power of the Holy Spirit.

Fields White Unto Harvest

We need each other in order to fulfill God's call on our lives. As we look at what the Lord is doing in Eastern Europe at the time of this writing, we see that now is the time for us in the Church of Jesus Christ to come into "the unity of the faith." (Eph. 4:13.)

I was blessed to be in Austria at the beginning of the mass exodus of East Germans into West Germany when that nation's Communist government lessened travel restrictions to the free world. It was beautiful to see how God had opened the Iron Curtain after all those years. I have never seen people so hungry for freedom as those people were. And thousands of them were also hungry for *God.*

For the first time in over forty years, there is some measure of freedom of religion in many areas of Eastern Europe. The Church must take advantage of the doors which have been so miraculously opened to the spread of the Gospel.

Several years ago my wife and I were in Hungary. When we got ready to minister at a local church, we had to walk out of the hotel and down to the street to make sure we were not being followed. Then we hurried a few blocks to a certain place where the pastor had arranged to pick us up. From there we secretly drove out to a farm house where we preached in an underground church. Now it seems that situation is changing.

I saw on television the opening of the border of Hungary. I watched as the barbwire was being taken down and rolled up. Now visitors can buy a piece of wire with an inscription on it which says: "A part of the Iron Curtain."

I wept as I thought: "If there was ever a time for us to get Bibles into that area, it's now."

God is saying to the Church, "Here is your opportunity."

Billy Graham was in Hungary during the month of August 1989. Over 120,000 people gathered in a stadium to hear him preach the Gospel. So many were saved, it was impossible to get literature to all of them individually, so it was taken and just thrown to the spiritually starved crowds. The ushers believed God that the literature would get to the ones who wanted and needed it most.

Can you see what God is doing in the earth? This move of the Holy Spirit is far greater than the charismatic movement. It's greater than the Baptist church, or the Assemblies of God, or any other single denomination or church group on earth. We Christians must link up together in a joint effort. We must come to understand our anointing, our authority, our assignment, and then begin to flow with each other and God's Spirit.

Vision in a Field

In 1977, while my wife and I were attending school, I didn't have any idea what God had for my life, so I began to seek the Lord. We lived in an apartment building which was located right beside a huge field. Every day, I would get up early in the morning and walk up and down that field, praying and seeking God's direction for my life. I didn't know anybody to help me, and I couldn't figure out how God was going to get me into the ministry.

One day as I was walking up and down that field, I looked toward some high weeds. Suddenly I saw faces of all kinds, shapes and colors: white faces, yellow faces, red faces, black faces. They were all over those weeds. As I gazed at that startling scene, suddenly the anointing of the Lord came upon me and I began to preach. I preached my heart out. I think I must have delivered the best sermon I have ever preached.

When I had finished, I gave an altar call, and people got saved, healed and delivered. A great revival took place right out in that empty field about six o'clock in the morning.

What had happened was that God had impregnated my spirit with a dream, a vision. From that time on, I knew I was going to carry the Gospel to the nations. I didn't have any idea how God was going to bring that vision to reality; I just knew that somehow He would.

My wife and I went on to graduate from school. Then we attended and graduated from Rhema Bible Training Center in Tulsa, Oklahoma. After our Bible studies, God supernaturally brought us to Little Rock, Arkansas, where we became associated with Agape Church.

In 1982, I began to see my vision come to pass. I started to travel overseas, making contact with people who were doing great things for God. That fall, we opened the Agape School for World Evangelism. My dream was becoming reality.

It was during this time that the Lord spoke to me from 1 Samuel 16:21. He told me to get my priorities into proper order. I learned that I was to be my pastor's armorbearer and to stand with him to fulfill the vision God had placed in his heart.

The Anointing of an Armorbearer

In order to develop the true spirit of an armorbearer, the first step is to understand our anointing. We have noted that an armorbearer is anointed to carry another man's shield into battle. His call and duty is to lay down his life for someone else.

In 2 Kings 3:11 we read: **But Jehoshaphat said, Is there not here a prophet of the Lord, that we may inquire of the Lord by him? And one of the king of Israel's servants answered and said, Here is Elisha the son of Shaphat, which poured water on the hands of Elijah.**

I believe that right now there are people who have been faithful to "pour water on the hands of their Elijah." You mark it down, the anointing of God is coming upon them. God is raising up all kinds of people, and the ones He is looking for are those who have shown themselves to be loyal servants, anointed as armorbearers.

The Word of the Lord may be with you, as it was with Elisha, because God looks at the heart. He looked at Elisha's heart, and the Word of the Lord was with him.

The Mantle of a Prophet

I wonder, if Elijah were alive today, how many people would be standing in line wanting to receive his mantle? I have a feeling Elijah would be very rough with them. I believe he would tell them, "Get your own mantle!"

Every true believer has his own mantle of anointing. We do not need to covet another man's mantle or anointing.

Elisha remained faithful to Elijah under all kinds of different circumstances. Historians tell us that Elisha served Elijah for about fifteen to twenty years. By this we know that Elisha heard everything that Elijah said, and saw everything he did, whether good or bad.

When King Ahab sent soldiers after Elijah, he was sitting on a hill. Elijah cried out to the captain of the guard, **...If I be a man of God, then let fire come down from heaven, and consume thee and thy fifty...**(2 Kings 1:10). The fire fell, and fifty men died, leaving fifty horses to go running back to town with empty saddles.

How would you have responded if you had been Elijah's associate at this time? You would have thought to yourself, "Boy, am I glad I'm on his side!" You would have been proud to tell everyone, "I work for Elijah."

Recognizing the Human Side of Leaders

In 1 Kings 18:17-40, we see another time that fire came down from heaven at Elijah's request. This time it was to consume a sacrifice offered to the Lord. We all remember the story of the famous contest on Mount Carmel between Elijah and the heathen prophets to prove which was the true God: Jehovah or Baal. After the Lord had sent fire from heaven to consume the sacrifice, His prophet, Elijah, took a sword and slew the four hundred prophets of Baal.

Following an experience like that, you would think that this man would not be afraid of anything. But we read that when the wicked Queen Jezebel sent a message threatening the life of Elijah, he became frightened and fled into the wilderness. (2 Kings 19:1-4.)

How do you respond when your leader reacts in fear, when you discover that he is human just as you are? As Elijah's associate, what would you have said to him? You would probably have stood and shouted to him as he ran, "Oh man of spirit and power, come back!" Here is an important question. Have you seen your leader fall? Have you seen him make a great mistake and even get into sin? What's your reaction? Are you ready to leave and find some other place of employment, or are you willing to help, support and see him restored? Here is where we really find out what we are made of. If there is a true attitude of repentance, a faithful man will stand with his leader. Proverbs 11:13 says, **A talebearer revealeth secrets: but he that is of a faithful spirit concealeth the matter.** A true armorbearer knows how to control his tongue in public, but how to speak boldly in prayer.

Elisha remained faithful to Elijah, and because of this faithfulness, when the time came for Elijah to leave this earth, Elisha could ask for a double portion of his anointing. (2 Kings 2:9.) Elijah knew the heart of the young man who had served him so well. He told Elisha that if he saw him when he left the earth, then his request would be granted. (v. 10.) When Elijah departed, Elisha was there to watch him being taken up into heaven in a fiery chariot. (v. 11.) Elijah's mantle fell from his shoulders at the feet of Elisha. It was then, at that time, that the anointing doubled.

In these last days, I expect to see a similar doubling, or even a tripling, of God's anointing upon His people. But it will come upon those who have been faithful to their Elijah. Whether you see your leader do great things, or make great mistakes, you must still remain faithful to him.

In Revelation 4:7, we see the four faces of Jesus:

> **And the first beast was like a lion, and the second beast like a calf, and the third beast had a face as a man, and the fourth was like a flying eagle.**

A lion, a calf, a man and an eagle. We see Jesus as a lion in dealing with the devil and sin. We see Him as a calf as He came to serve humanity. We see Him as a man as He held the little children and blessed them. And we see Him as an eagle as He prayed, preached and healed the people.

In every leader you will see a lion, when it comes to dealing with a problem; a calf, when it comes to serving people; a man, when it comes to tending the sheep; and as an eagle, when it comes to standing up to minister the Word of the Lord. But you will also see your leader as a man when he is hurt and wounded.

Most people only see their leader as an eagle, but you will see your leader in all four faces. You will see him when he is less than full of faith and power, when he says something or does something that may offend you, when things are tight financially and you have to cut back the budget of your department.

It is easy to respect your pastor when he is functioning as an eagle under God's anointing. But you must also respect him when times are hard and he is operating more as a man. Respect is due the leader no matter how he may appear or feel.

Some people have the mistaken idea that those who work in the ministry sit around all day, praying in tongues and prophesying to one another. The ministry, however, is *work, work* and more *work*. It requires an ability to work with other people without giving or taking offense. True armorbearing is the ability to see the human side of our leaders and still maintain respect for them.

Recognizing the Right of Divine Authority

The second area that we must come to understand in order to be true armorbearers is the right of divine authority. We must know, recognize and yield to God's authority in our lives. We have to pray daily, "Father, not my will, but Thine be done." We have to be determined in our hearts to stay in God's will regardless of the cost or consequences.

When we look at Jesus, we might think that because He was the Son of God He had no problem at all in fulfilling God's will for His life. Let's look at Hebrews 5:7,8 to see if this is true:

> **Who in the days of his flesh, when he had offered up prayers and supplications with *strong crying* and *tears* unto him that was able to save him from death, and was heard in that he feared;**
>
> **Though he were a Son, yet learned he obedience by the things which he suffered.**

We see Jesus in "strong crying and tears" before the Father, yet choosing to remain in God's will for His life and praying to fulfill the divine call that was upon Him.

Whatever it takes, whether you are happy or hurting, make a firm commitment in your heart to fulfill God's plan for your life.

Several years ago the Lord said something to me that has helped me during hard times. He said: "Keep your eyes on the resurrection, and you can endure the cross." The cross is not a burden; it's the call of God on our lives. If it is God's will for you to stay in one place for the rest of your life in order to give yourself to and for someone else, then let God's will be done.

Giving Birth to God's Will

One day I was thinking of what God has placed in my heart to do for Him. I have a God-ordained desire to see churches and Bible schools raised up in all nations around the world. I asked the Lord one time, "Father, how is this vision going to ever come into reality?"

He said to me: "Son, you are going to have to bring it forth by *intimacy, pregnancy, travail,* and *birth.*"

Spiritual birth takes place the same way that natural birth occurs. In order to bring forth in the spiritual realm, we have to get intimate with God. From that intimacy comes pregnancy. From pregnancy will eventually come travail, and then, finally, birth.

We must give birth to the fulfillment of God's will in our lives. The fulfillment of our God-given vision will not drop down on us out of the sky. We must draw nigh to God, and then He will draw nigh to us. (James 4:8.)

Some of the most miserable people in this world are women who are are pregnant and overdue. Likewise, some of the most miserable Christians in the world are those who are "pregnant" with a vision from God, and yet have not been able to give birth to that vision. But intimacy with God must come first, before there can ever be a pregnancy.

I believe that today the Holy Spirit is speaking the words of Hosea 10:12 to the Body of Christ: **Sow to yourselves in righteousness, reap in mercy; break up your fallow ground:** *for it is time to seek the Lord,* **till he come and rain righteousness upon you.**

To become intimate with the Lord, we must seek Him with our whole heart.

Once we have developed an intimate relationship with God, we will get pregnant with a dream or a vision which has been planted in us by the Lord. Then we must take that vision which has been supernaturally planted in us by God and begin to nurture it, causing to it to grow and develop. Sooner or later it will lead to godly travail, without which there can be no birth. That travail is our intercession.

Isaiah 40:3 speaks of: **The voice of him that crieth in the wilderness, Prepare ye the way of the Lord, make straight in the desert a highway for our God.**

John the Baptist was the forerunner of Jesus. He prepared the way for Jesus' first coming. You and I are preparing the way for the Lord's second coming.

One day the Lord revealed Isaiah 40:3 to me in this way: "The voice of him that crieth in Little Rock, Arkansas, prepare ye the way of the Lord, make straight in Little Rock a highway for our God."

Intercession is like building a highway for the Lord. We have to do the the work first, and then God will send His glory. If we will be patient and faithful, if we will follow the process of intimacy, pregnancy, travail and birth, we will see the fulfillment of our heavenly dream and vision.

Following God's Predetermined Course

...being predestinated according to the purpose of him who worketh all things after the counsel of his own will.

Ephesians 1:11

The word translated **predestinated** in this verse means "predetermined." God has a predetermined, predesigned course for everyone of us. That course was set before we were ever born into this earth.

The Lord has said to each of us: **Before I formed thee in the belly I knew thee...**(Jer. 1:5.) God knew you and me before the foundation of the world, and He set an individual course for each of us to follow. Now it is up to you and me to discover God's course for us and to follow that course so that we may give spiritual birth to the dream and vision He has had in mind for us from before the creation of the world.

I know that, at this time, I am called to be an armorbearer to my pastor. And because I am determined to stay in God's will, every promise in God's Word can be fulfilled in my life.

The Apostle Paul said, **I have fought a good fight, I have finished my course...**(2 Tim. 4:7). Paul fought to stay on course, and he made it. He finished the course laid out for him by God.

Discover what your course is, and then stay with it and never give up until you have reached your God-ordained destination and goal.

Understanding Our Assignment and Appreciating Our Gifts

The last important step we need to take is to learn and understand our God-given assignment. The fulfillment of that assignment is dependent upon the proper use of the divine gifts which have been bestowed upon us.

Every year my family gets together on Christmas Eve. Because my family is so large, prior to Christmas we draw names to see who we will buy presents for. One Christmas, while handing out the gifts, I noticed that my twin brother had received two presents. His name had accidentally been placed on two different gifts. When I opened my present, I was disappointed in what I got. I looked at my twin brother and he was laughing because he had received two nice gifts. Seeing my disappointed expression, my wife came over to console me.

"Don't worry, Terry," she said, "when we get back home, we will exchange it for something you like better."

Now the very same thing happens in the Body of Christ. We open the gifts God has given us, and we run to someone else to see what he got. Then we hurry to another to see what gift he has received. When we look at our gift from the Lord, we are unhappy with it and immediately think to ourselves, "I know what I'll do; I'll swap it for something I like better."

This is why there are so many people running around in church circles today claiming to be an apostle or a prophet or a teacher. Many times what they are really doing is "gift swapping," because they do not like the spiritual gift which God has bestowed upon them.

We must know in our hearts that we had absolutely nothing to do with choosing the gifts that God has placed inside of each of us. He bestows gifts according to His will, and it is up to us to receive those gifts and allow the Lord to add to us more gifts "as He wills." (1 Cor. 12:11.)

> **But now hath God set the members every one of them in the body, as it hath pleased him.**
> **1 Corinthians 12:18**

As we are faithful in the small things, God will make us rulers over many. (Matt. 25:21.) As we stay with the assignment and the gifts God has given each of us, He will bring our gift before great men.

I remember one day while attending Bible school, I saw a fellow I knew come into class all dressed up. This was unusual because he generally wore jeans. When I asked him why he was so dressed up, he answered, "Because all the 'big shots' from the denominational headquarters are coming to school today; just stick with me and I'll introduce you to the really big ones."

I got so mad I went to my room and told the Lord that if that was how the ministry works, then He could count me out of it. The Lord said so clearly to me that day, "Son, don't you realize that you have already been introduced to the Big One"?

That's right. They don't come any "bigger" than God. Stay with your individual assignment, and in due time the Lord will exalt you.

I went through a time when I saw God begin to do many great things in my life. It was a time of the manifestation and fulfillment of many dreams and visions. During this period, I started experiencing more problems and having more frequent confrontations than ever before in my life. As director of our Bible and mission school, I felt like a fireman. As soon as one "blaze" was extinguished, another would crop up somewhere else. It seemed as if everything I did was wrong.

Now on the one hand, God was doing great things, but on the other hand I felt run down and discouraged. At this time I thought to myself, "I will just let my wife (who is the administrator of the school) start doing more; I'll go to the mission field where the work is fun and I can just send back picture postcards."

Now my mind was made up to do that until, while in prayer, I saw in my spirit a vision of David being anointed by Samuel. I saw the oil running down his head as he was anointed king of Israel. At that time, the Lord asked me this question: "What did David do after he was anointed king?"

I thought for a moment and answered, "He went back to tending his father's sheep in the field."

The Lord spoke to me: "Had David gone out looking for a giant to kill at this time, the lion and the bear would have eaten his flock. That school is your flock, so you had better see to it."

"Yes, Sir," I said, "I see that very clearly."

Whether we are a pastor, an associate pastor, a music director or a layman, each of us has a flock. That flock belongs to us individually, and God expects us to tend it. David's flock was his assignment from God, and he knew that, although he had been anointed to be king of Israel, his first priority right at the moment was to continue to tend to his first assignment.

You see, the giants will come. But, if you will stay with your assignment, when the time comes you will meet and conquer your giant just as David met and overcame his. Like David, you will be exalted, *after* you have first proven yourself faithful.

I knew personally that if I did not take the time to put myself into the students under my care, I could not expect them to flow with me once they had reached the mission field.

You may look at your current condition and position and wonder how God could ever use you. You may think to yourself: "I am not the person in charge, so I have to stay submitted to other people. How will I ever get to fulfill my own dream and vision?" Be at peace and know that God's Word is not written for leaders only. It is written for the Body of Christ, and that includes you — right where you are today.

The Mission of the Church in the Last Days

Recently I was in Austria and was talking with a national pastor. He shared with me something that blessed me greatly.

In 1987, when I was in that country, I was scheduled to lead a Bible conference. I struggled within myself as to what to teach. I rose up early the day before the conference and said to the Lord, "Father, what do You want me to teach?" I had not consulted with Him about His direction.

The Lord said, "Preach on the pattern of the New Testament church."

I began reading through the book of Acts to discover what that pattern was. The theme of all the messages I received was: "If Austria is going to be won to God, it must be done through the local church."

I realized then that God was saying, "Today is the day of the local church in Austria." I believe that is true of the whole world.

This Austrian pastor shared with me how as a result of that one conference, four local churches had been started in four different areas. I was so blessed and moved in my heart that God had used me to affect a nation. It had happened because I was obedient and taught what He wanted taught.

In 1989, we opened the first Full-Gospel Bible school in the history of that European nation. I have found God to be so faithful to us as we determine to *walk in our anointing,* to *stay in submission to His divine authority,* and to *fulfill our God-ordained assignment.* It takes an understanding of all these areas in order to be an armorbearer.

Ours could very well be the generation that rises to meet Jesus in the air. It is time for us to re-evaluate our lives, and our ministries, to make sure that we are where we need to be and doing what we need to be doing. Satan does not mind our building our dreams and visions, as long as he is the head contractor. If what we are doing is not of the Spirit and directed by Him, any edifice we erect is going to fall. (Ps. 127:1.) Satan will allow us to build, making sure that we smear God's name all over our own dreams and visions, so that when they fail it will appear that God has failed.

When we set out to build the Kingdom, we must be sure that God is one hundred percent in and behind what we are doing.

The spirit of an armorbearer is the Spirit of Christ. This is the day we see that God's children should take up the shields of others and be willing to carry them forth into battle. We have an overall vision and mandate from God to reach our generation. This can be accomplished when we develop the spirit of an armorbearer and truly begin to give of ourselves.

The armorbearers of today will be the leaders of tomorrow.

God's Armorbearer Volume 1 was written to give you an understanding of the roll of the Armorbearer to his leader.

Over the years I have been accused by a few of trying to take an Old Testament office and making it New Testament. The key to explaining that is that the Armorbearer is not an office it is an attitude. Every one in the Local Church should carry the spirit of an Armorbearer. It is the heart of a servant. To be the greatest in the Kingdom is to be a servant of all.

God's Armorbearer Volume 2 is designed to give you the keys to staying faithful in your calling to your leader. It is one thing to have the revelation of an Armorbearer but it is another thing to stand and live it day after day. In Volume 2 we will deal with Longevity, Commitment, Attitude, and Teamwork.

My prayer is that the Holy Spirit will impart into you an Armorbearer spirit with the stability to stand during the good times and the hard.

Always remember that what you make happen for someone else God will make happen for you.

God's Armorbearer II
How To Bloom Where God Has Planted You

by
Terry Nance

God's Armorbearer II
How To Bloom Where God Has Planted You

by
Terry Nance

God's Armorbearer II
How To Bloom Where God Has Planted You
ISBN 0-97191-930-5
Copyright © 1994 by Terry Nance
Focus on the Harvest
P.O. Box 241546
Little Rock, AR 72223

Dedication

I dedicate *God's Armorbearer II* to my dad, Tommy Nance, who taught me the importance of being on time, keeping my word, and staying with a job until it was finished. He has played an important part in my life and ministry.

Also, I extend special thanks to the Agape Church Staff who through their diligence and experience provided the keys used in this book.

Contents

Foreword   9

1. The Hour of the Local Church   11

2. Keys to Longevity   19

3. Keys to Commitment   37

4. Keys to Attitude   43

5. Keys to Teamwork   57

Foreword

Several years ago, we were one of the host churches for the Billy Graham team when they came to town to prepare for a crusade in Little Rock.

I remember being introduced to the man who addressed our steering committee. He said that he was one of the youngest crusade directors on Dr. Graham's team. He had only been with the ministry twenty years.

Later, we hosted a meeting at our church, where Cliff Barrows spoke and George Beverly Shea sang. As we all sat in our guest room before the service, they began reminiscing and talking about the "forty-plus" years they had been with Billy Graham. It was so precious to hear them laugh as they remembered the funny things, and yet at the same time, it was powerful to hear of the faithfulness to their call.

In Paul's charge to Timothy, as he finished his course and kept the faith, he charged Timothy to be diligent in coming to him. Then he began to share about those who had forsaken him and had done him much evil: **Demas has forsaken me, having loved this present world . . . only Luke is with me. Take Mark and bring him with you: for he is profitable to me for the ministry** (2 Tim. 4:7-11).

At this writing, Terry Nance and I have been together fifteen years. I suppose Terry has done everything there is to do in the growth of a church. He always was faithful to "bloom where he was planted." The Bible says a faithful man will abound in blessings. He is fulfilling his calling in this ministry and is a blessing to the world through our Agape School of World Evangelism, of which he is the dean of students. Terry and his wife, Kim, are two of the finest people we have ever known, and I know his second book on the ministry of an armorbearer will impart a spirit of excellence to your life.

Happy Caldwell
Pastor, Agape Church
Little Rock, Arkansas

1
The Hour of the Local Church

From the prophetic signs happening every day, it seems Jesus is soon to return. That is why I feel such an urgency about each member of the Body of Christ finding his place and remaining faithful, so we can be productive in God's Kingdom. I believe this is the hour of the local church.

The local church is the *hub* from which all ministry gifts are to function and the center out of which they are to flow. In the local church, you find what is needed to build the character of Christ in us. Each member of the Body of Christ should discover his or her gift and calling, and then become fully connected to a local church, submitting one to another and submitting to the God-called pastors and leaders there.

When people come into my office desiring to become part of our local church body, my first question always is, "What church do you come from, and who was your pastor?"

You can tell what type of Christian you are dealing with by the answer you get. Millions of Christians attend church services only on Sunday mornings and are not committed physically or spiritually to that church. Their reasons for attending range from tradition to religious duty to social acceptance in the community. Going to church once a week eases their consciences of religious obligations.

Think what could happen in this country if those people would get on fire for God and begin to release their gifts and talents in the Body! We would see the world reached with the Gospel. The local church is called to touch its community, town, or city for God. To the reader, I would ask these questions:

- What part are you to play?
- Where can you get involved?
- What resources do you have available?
- What opportunities lie before you?
- What do the leaders of your local church need from you?
- How many times have they asked for help, or how many times have you volunteered?

Take a look at what you have to offer your local church. You may feel that you have nothing to offer, but that is never true of anyone. Each born-again believer has something to offer that is unique. Each Christian has a call on his life which will become apparent once he is involved in a church.

First Peter 4:10 (AMP) says:

> As each of you has received a gift (a particular spiritual talent, a gracious divine endowment), employ it for one another as [befits] good trustees of God's many-sided grace —faithful stewards of the extremely diverse [powers and gifts granted to Christians by] unmerited favor.

Once you read that verse, there are no more excuses. You have a talent that your pastor and your local church needs to help reach your city. Each church has a vision that was given to the pastor by the Holy Spirit, and the pastor should take the time to share that vision with the church. Then members of the congregation should seek the Lord Jesus Christ to discover where each of them fits into that vision.

Opportunities to get involved are unlimited. Most local churches have departments, activities, or outreach ministries in which each church member would fit. Listed below are some of the departments available in our local church:

Academy	Maintenance
School of World Evangelism	Marriage Builders
Bookstore	Music Ministry
Children's Ministry	Prison Ministry
Counseling	Publications
Counselors in Service	Security
Disciples Training Classes	Singles Life I (20-24)
Evangelism Ministry	Singles Life II (25-39)
Financial Counseling	Singles Life III (40-60)
Door Greeters	Sound Department
Helping Hands	Tape Duplication
Hospital Visitation	Temporarily Impaired
Housekeeping	TV-KVTN (Channel 25)
Intercession	Ushers
Jail Ministry	Visitation
"Kids Like You"	Visitor Center
Ladies Bible Study	

Other churches may offer more or fewer avenues of Christian work, but there are always opportunities available that require people willing to release their talents.

Armorbearers Are Vital for Churches

Without those who do this, the church cannot function, and the Gospel will not be preached to our cities. Pastors and leaders in the majority of churches have been bearing the brunt of the work of the ministry. That is why you hear of so many ministers "burning out."

Pastors and other spiritual leaders should be *breaking through*, not burning out. Spiritual and natural breakthroughs will happen as the Body of Christ decides to do its full part.

I came to Agape Church in Little Rock two weeks after it was started in May of 1979. As soon as I arrived, I began to get involved. I set out to do whatever I could do to help Pastor Happy Caldwell fulfill his vision for the church.

In 1982, we started a mission school to reach around the world. My call was to direct that school and place missionaries wherever the Lord led. One night in 1983, the Lord quickened my heart to read the story of David and Saul. I turned to 1 Samuel 16:21 and read:

> **And David came to Saul, and stood before him: and he loved him greatly; and he became his armourbearer.**

At that time, the Lord said to me, "Son, I have called you to be Pastor Caldwell's armorbearer."

An armorbearer carried his leader's shield into battle, and if necessary, he laid down his life for the one whom he served. The shield for me is the vision God birthed into Pastor Caldwell's life.

The Lord said, "Run with the vision I have given him, and I will see to it that yours will be fulfilled."

I am now in my fifteenth year in this ministry, and I am seeing God faithfully fulfill His call on my life. I am blooming where God has planted me.

God is calling for many Christians to become armorbearers for their leaders and for each other. We should begin to work as a team to advance God's Kingdom in the earth.

While preparing to speak to our office and ministerial staff one day, the Holy Spirit put into my heart to ask them each to give me two keys that had produced longevity in their positions and had helped them bloom where they were planted. We have several full-time staff members who have been with the church for many years. The church staff overall has remained very solidly committed.

From that meeting came forty keys to producing longevity of service in the place where God has placed you. Here are those keys in the order in which they were given.

Successful Keys to Blooming Where You Are Planted

1. You must have a call from God.

2. First of all, make sure you have a real personal relationship with Christ.

3. Ask God to give you His vision, or goal for your life.

4. Be willing to do whatever is asked.

5. Do not lose sight of the people behind the work.

6. Be thankful for your position and never take it for granted.

7. Be willing to submit to authority.

8. Know that you are in God's will.

9. Know that your rewards are laid up in Heaven.

10. Develop a servant's heart.

11. Walk without offense.

12. Serve as if you were serving Jesus Himself, and do not get your eyes on the man under whom you work. On the other hand, be careful to respect the call that is on his life.

13. Be patient.

14. Have a loyalty that goes beyond personal feelings.

15. Respect everyone.

16. Hear no evil, see no evil, and speak no evil.

17. Judge yourself.

18. Do not ever be too big to do the small things or too small to do the big things.

19. Commit to the ministry the way you ought to be committed to your marriage.

20. Know that you are important and needed.

21. Help other people fulfill their ministries.

22. Do everything you know to do to get where you want to be.

23. Do the very best wherever you are.

24. Stay with something until the job is done.

25. Never quit.

26. Be dependable.

27. Be a good follower as well as a good leader.

28. Maintain your joy in the Lord.

29. Always remain sensitive to the Holy Spirit.

30. Always obey God's specific instructions.

31. Be patient with one another.

32. Always walk in love.

33. Be willing to change direction.

34. Know that God is your Source.

35. Use all the abilities that God has given you.

36. Have a healthy perspective of yourself.

37. Always keep the overall vision of the church before you.

38. Maintain a good attitude.

39. Trust in God's grace and His anointing on your life.

40. Be big enough to be rebuked and corrected.

I have divided these forty keys into four separate categories that will help us get a better understanding of them. We will take a look at the most important keys of each category:

- Longevity
- Commitment
- Attitude
- Teamwork

As I begin to share about these four areas, I will be presenting this from the viewpoint of blooming in the local church. These things are what it will take for you to be faithful and to be where God wants you to be. These are working in my life, and I know they will work in yours.

2

Keys to Longevity

The first key to longevity is *understanding the call of God.*

Matthew 13:37,38 says:

> **He answered and said unto them, He that soweth the good seed is the Son of man;**
>
> **The field is the world; the good seed are the children of the kingdom . . . .**

You can see that in God's hands, we are "seed," and the world is His field. He wants us to put our lives in His hands and let Him plant us into the world. God determined the type of seed you are and where you were to be planted.

Genesis 1:11 says that the "seed is in itself." Now, what does that mean? It means that a seed of corn is always going to produce only corn, a kernel of wheat will produce wheat, a grain of rice will produce rice. You cannot get rice from corn. So it is in the mind of God. He planned our lives before the world was created. Now, He wants to plant each of us so we can begin to bloom and bring forth fruit in season.

If you take a quick look at how a seed produces, it will give you some spiritual insight. A seed first is planted in the ground to go through a process of actually dying. Then, a rootlet will begin to push its way through the earth as the rain and sunshine give life to it.

Does that seed ever think, "Am I going to get through all of this dirt on top of me? It is so hard, and I feel hopeless."

· But then, one day, it happens. The seed comes forth, and the bud breaks into the sunlight. Many members of the Body of Christ are like that seed — all they see is dirt piled on top of them. Even staff members of ministries sometimes feel mistreated and left out. Perhaps they feel God has forsaken them because all they can see is dirt.

If they will just stay where God planted them and be faithful during the hard times, they will come forth. A seed is destined to spring forth if it is planted in good soil. If you know you are in the will of God and are where He wants you to be, then you *will* come forth, because it is God's destiny at work in you.

God wants His children to grow up and be like trees planted by rivers of water. (Ps. 1:3.) Have you ever noticed something peculiar about a tree? *It never moves!* We have beautiful pine trees on our church property, but I have never driven into the parking lot and found one of those trees had moved overnight to a different place because it did not like where it was planted.

Yet, in the Body of Christ and even on church staffs, the first time someone is offended, he pulls up his roots and moves somewhere else — then wonders why there is no fruit in his life.

If a tree is continually uprooted and replanted, eventually the roots will die. Many Christians have experienced this. Because of rebellion and sin in their hearts, they constantly jump from one church to another. They refuse to submit to authority, or they feel they have special gifts for the church which the pastor is not willing to recognize.

That kind of attitude keeps a person from fulfilling the divine, Heaven-ordained call God placed on his life. We must judge ourselves and be willing to die to our own purposes and dreams to let God's will be done, no matter the personal cost.

Second Timothy 1:9 says:

Who hath saved us, and called us with a holy calling, not according to our works, but according to his own purpose and grace, which was given us in Christ Jesus before the world began.

This, to me, is one of the most important scriptures in the Bible as far as understanding your calling. God has saved us and called us. That means if you are born again, you are called. You cannot stand before Jesus one day and say, "I was never called." He saved you and called you, according to His own purpose and grace.

God Has a Purpose for You

God has a purpose in life for you to fulfill. You are not here by accident. You have a destiny in God to fulfill. You must find out your purpose by seeking God. Then, you become the deciding factor in fulfilling that purpose.

It was the God-ordained, God-destined time for the children of Israel to go into the promised land when God took them there from Egypt. However, because of doubt and unbelief, they missed their purpose in life.

For forty years, the Israelites walked in circles in the wilderness until all of the males older than twenty years had died. People with no purposes tend to walk in circles, blaming their failures on God or someone else. They walk until they dig holes for themselves and eventually die. Then, many times, they die full of bitterness, mad at other people and God.

Joshua and Caleb, the only two men of that generation to live to see the promised land, were of a different spirit. They knew they had a purpose and a call on their lives and that, by faith in God, they could possess the land.

I really feel sorry for Joshua and Caleb because they had to wait forty years to take what rightfully belonged to them.

They could have been enjoying their destiny, but they had to wait because of the rebellion of others.

Second Timothy 1:9 says God's purpose and grace was given to us in Christ before the world ever began. God knew who you were before you were born. Before He ever said, "Light be," He knew you in His omnipotent mind. He had a reason for your being born in the generation in which you were born.

I got real honest with God one day, and I asked Him while in prayer, "I want to know why I am here? I want to know why I was born into the Nance family? Why am I here at this time?"

You see, you had nothing to do with it. God did not ask your opinion when He planned you and made you. It was all up to Him. Why were we not born in the days of Abraham, Moses, David, or even Jesus? Why were we not born in the fifteenth, sixteenth, or seventeenth centuries? Why did God put us in this last generation?

I believe, when God created the world, He saw a time period in which sin would abound as never before, a time when great calamities would happen on the earth. He foresaw a time when the greatest deception would come to try the people of God, and a time when gross darkness would come on many people, and the love of many would wax cold.

In the midst of seeing all this, I believe God said to Himself, "I am going to raise up a people who will not compromise My Word, a people with My Spirit, anointing, and joy to go forth in those days and usher in the greatest move of My Spirit the world has ever seen. I will pour out My Spirit upon all flesh and raise up a glorious Church without spot or wrinkle." (Eph. 5:27.)

When God determined these things, He said it would be a "special" people to live in these days, and in His mind,

He saw *you*. He saw you and put you in place for a divine purpose.

No matter what position you hold, you are there to produce for the Kingdom of God and bring the lost into the saving knowledge of Jesus. We must realize that we were called before we met our families, our spouses, or anyone else in our lives. And we must, at the Judgment, give account to God for what we did with that purpose and calling.

> **For we must all appear before the judgment seat of Christ; that everyone may receive the things done in his body, according to that he hath done, whether it be good or bad.**
>
> **2 Corinthians 5:10**

It is an awesome thing to think that I will stand before Jesus and give an account of what I did with the gifts and calling on my life. My pastor will not be able to stand up for me and say that I was a good associate. My wife will not be able to testify that I was a good husband. Only I can answer the Lord.

He will say, "Terry, what did you do with what I gave you. Did you fulfill your assignment?"

My assignment at this point is to be the senior associate and missions director of Agape Church, Inc. The Lord has told me to take the same vision, anointing, and integrity of this church and reproduce it in the world.

All Will Give An Account

To you who are reading this book, I say by the Spirit of God, "As surely as you are reading this, you too will stand before Him and answer the same questions."

That is why our callings are so important and why we must endure hardships if they come while fulfilling them. We must be determined to have God's will in our lives no matter the cost. Hebrews 5:7 says:

**Who in the days of his flesh, when he had offered
up prayers and supplications with strong crying and
tears unto him that was able to save him from death,
and was heard in that he feared.**

Jesus went through strong crying and tears to fulfill
God's will. Many church and ministry staff personnel run
from anything that is hard and say, if it is the will of God, it
would be easy! Well, welcome to the real world. It takes
strong crying and tears sometimes to stay where God
plants you and refuse to move no matter the conditions.

In building longevity in your life, another priority is
your *personal relationship with Christ*. It is easy to stay so
involved with the work of the ministry that our lives seem
to be racing ahead of us. It is easy to be so caught up with
the work of the ministry that we overlook our intimate
times with Jesus.

I find it very interesting that in Luke 11:1, the disciples
asked Jesus to teach them how to pray. Jesus' ministry was
very well-known at that time, with miracles, signs, and
wonders occurring all of the time. However, the Bible never
says that the disciples even one time asked Jesus for His
anointing.

Today, we see great men of God flowing in major
healing and deliverance anointings. It is amazing how
many people I hear who desire, covet, want — and would
do anything — if these ministers would lay hands on them
and "transfer" the anointing.

No one alive has ever flowed in the gifts of the Holy
Spirit to the degree that Jesus did. If we covet that kind of
anointing, we must do as the disciples did and ask Jesus
how to pray. We must follow the pattern set by Jesus.
Ministers are falling because they lost their intimacy with
the Lord. Many have fallen into sin simply because they
substituted work of the ministry for an intimate
relationship.

When in prayer one day, the Lord revealed to me the key to seeing the calling on my life fulfilled. It is by intimacy, pregnancy, travail, and birth. Spiritual life is born into the earth following the same pattern as natural life is born. We must become "intimate" with God. From that intimacy comes "pregnancy."

That means we are pregnant with the visions and plans God has for our lives. Then, we must travail. *To travail* means "to intercede, care for, pray, and speak God's Word over that vision or plan. The travailing comes first; then, the children are born.

We get God's plan, will, and direction by establishing a habit of prayer and study of the Word. Pressures are coming at Christians today in a greater intensity than we have ever experienced. That is because the devil knows his time is short. The key to our being able to walk in victory is to cry out, "Lord, teach us to pray."

Those Who Seek God Will Follow a Vision

You will have many opportunities to quit the position you hold. I have had times of trial and hardship when I prayed for God to let me leave! And I found that the strength to stand, strength to go on, and strength to resist Satan only comes in prayer. In our quiet times with God, He gives peace and strength.

We must develop a heart that seeks after God. David, King of Israel, was known as a man whose heart followed after God. If we could interview him today, we might ask what his greatest goal was in life:

- Was it to be the greatest king?

- Was it to be the greatest musician?

- Was it to be the wealthiest man on earth?

David's answer would be one of his psalms:

25

> One thing have I desired of the Lord, that will I
> seek after; that I may dwell in the house of the Lord all
> the days of my life, to behold the beauty of the Lord,
> and to inquire in his temple.
>
> **Psalm 27:4**

David's quest in life was to have God's heart. If we are ever to be true successes in God's Kingdom, we also must know that our first ministry is to glorify and honor Him. First Peter 2:5 says that we are a holy priesthood, and we are to offer up spiritual sacrifices, acceptable to God by Christ Jesus.

The first calling for all of us is to worship and honor the Lord on a daily basis. Jesus prayed to the Father. He had a habit of prayer. That was the key to His anointing, wisdom, and longevity.

> And he came out, and went, as he was wont (as was
> his habit) to the mount of Olives (to pray); and his
> disciples followed him.
>
> **Luke 22:39**

Another important part of longevity is *having a vision and a goal*. I heard a man say, "I would rather have high goals and reach half of them than to have no goals and reach all of them."

Second Kings 4:1-3 says:

> Now there cried a certain woman of the wives of
> the sons of the prophets unto Elisha, saying, Thy
> servant my husband is dead; and thou knowest that thy
> servant did fear the Lord: and the creditor is come to
> take unto him my two sons to be bondmen.
>
> And Elisha said unto her, What shall I do for thee?
> tell me, what hast thou in the house? And she said,
> Thine handmaid hath not anything in the house, save a
> pot of oil.
>
> Then he said, Go, borrow thee vessels abroad of all
> thy neighbors, even empty vessels; borrow not a few.

That widow was left with a choice: She could go and get a lot of vessels, or she could borrow just a few. She gathered vessels and began to pour the oil. When did the oil stop? It stopped when she ran out of jars. She held the key to her miracle.

She could have said, "It is too hot today to gather jars," or, "Elisha, I don't feel well," or "I could only find one jar."

Whatever she brought in is what she received. If she had really known what God was about to do, she could have found a dry well and said, "That is my jar!"

Elisha would have laughed, and I believe God would have laughed as well. If you do not exercise faith in life to reach a goal or vision, you will never achieve it. You are going to have to get up and work toward your goal. God blesses what you do.

When I first came on staff at Agape, I did not know exactly what my goal and vision was for God. I knew that I had a desire for the mission field but that was all. As I was becoming part of a new church, I could not expect to be sent immediately to the mission field. So I began by just locking and unlocking the church building and getting things ready before every service.

That was a small goal but still a responsibility God gave me to do, and I did that for three years until He raised up a full-time person to take care of it. In the meantime, doors to the mission field began to open. *You must start with what your hand finds to do.* (Eccl. 9:10.)

If you will go to your pastor or church leaders and begin to serve them, the vision God has for you will begin to come to pass. Be a blessing in your local church, and you will find doors opening up in all directions.

Everyone in some way must be connected with a local body under the leadership of a God-called pastor in the days to come. Many people move from one ministry to the next, based on what they think each has to offer them — never asking what God wants.

Stay Where God Puts You

Knowing that you are in the ministry that God intends for you is yet another key to longevity. I believe this is the decade of the local church. Using ministries as stepping stones is wrong, and that could be the reason you are not prospering in your call. This key applies to everyone, not just full-time ministers.

When I graduated from Southwestern Assembly of God Bible College, I received a very good offer. The dean of the college told me that he wanted to recommend me to a very good church that would have been a great opportunity. However, I had real peace in my heart about attending Rhema Bible Training Center in Broken Arrow, Oklahoma, near Tulsa.

I knew that, if we moved to Tulsa, it would mean both my wife and I would have to find jobs. This move would be a real test of faith for us, especially when I had the opportunity to move immediately into full-time ministry.

Friends would say, "Why are you going to a Bible school? You just graduated from college!"

But God had another plan. He was preparing my way to Little Rock via Tulsa. We must follow our hearts and not the offers. God holds the future, and the best future for you does not always hold what seems to be the best offer. The will of God is to stay planted where God has you until He says to move.

This leads to another key to longevity, which is *making God your complete Source*. Every Christian will be faced with a situation in which to make a decision to either trust God or to trust man. Jeremiah 17:5-8 says:

Thus saith the Lord; Cursed be the man that trusteth in man, and maketh flesh his arm, and whose heart departeth from the Lord.

For he shall be like the heath in the desert, and shall not see when good cometh; but shall inhabit the parched places in the wilderness, in a salt land and not inhabited.

Blessed is the man that trusteth in the Lord, and whose hope the Lord is.

For he shall be as a tree planted by the waters, and that spreadeth out her roots by the river, and shall not see when heat cometh, but her leaf shall be green; and shall not be careful in the year of drought, neither shall cease from yielding fruit.

We did move to Tulsa and rented a small apartment. My wife, Kim, got a job, and I worked part-time as youth director in a church. But we were barely making it. At one time, for two weeks, all we had in the house was about eight dozen eggs given us by Kim's aunt. The bills were paid, but we had no money for food.

When I realized that we had to eat eggs for two weeks, I wanted to cry for help from my mom and dad. I knew all I had to do was pick up the phone and the money would be on its way. However, I also knew that would be trusting in my parents and not in God.

After a few days, I thought that I would sprout feathers: We had fried eggs, scrambled eggs, boiled eggs, and poached eggs. Then I got a call from the pastor of a church with about a thousand members asking me to come work for him. The salary looked like a heaven-sent one, and I thought perhaps God wanted me to leave Tulsa and take that job.

I told the pastor I would come and visit with him about the job, but when I hung up the phone, Kim began to cry.

She said, "Terry, you know God wants us here. We can't even go down there and talk to the pastor about this."

After we prayed, I had to call the pastor back and apologize for even offering to come visit him about that job. I told him I knew God had called me to be in Tulsa. Then I hung up, looked at Kim, and said, "Pass the eggs."

I do not regret that decision, because that is how God taught me to trust Him. Even when I arrived in Little Rock and talked with the Caldwells, we knew it was a step of faith. They knew we were supposed to join them, and Kim and I knew God was telling us to come. We came with no mention of salary, just knowing by the inner peace that God would supply, and He has.

You must have a revelation in your heart that your church is not your source, your pastor is not your source, and your salary is not your source. Every Christian will face times when it is necessary to find out who to trust: God or man. If you lean toward man, then man will be the limit of your supply.

I have known people who volunteered to help in a local church, working for no pay but doing it unto the Lord. Then, because of their faithfulness, they were placed on staff. Now they were getting paid but were expected to be on time and put in a full day's work. Their attitudes began to be that the church owed them something. They felt they were worth more than they were paid, and the work demands were too much. They lost sight of Who they were working for and Who was their real Source.

Do not allow anger to rise up in you against your pastor or your employer when you find yourself in a situation where you must believe God financially. If you agreed to work for the salary offered by the ministry, you have no right to get angry when you face a situation of lack.

Your source of supply must be God.

Trust and Obey

Two other keys for longevity are *trusting in God's grace on your life* and *always obey God's original instructions.*

You have a grace on your life and talents and abilities to do what God has called you to do. You may not understand or realize your talents at first, but eventually, if you persist, you will see them.

First Corinthians 15:10 says:

But by the grace of God I am what I am: and his grace which was bestowed upon me was not in vain; but I laboured more abundantly than they all: yet not I, but the grace of God which was with me.

When I first came to work at Agape Church and sat down with Pastor Caldwell, he asked me what my talents were. I was embarrassed and really had nothing to say. As far as I knew, I had little talent.

So I looked at him and said, "The only thing I can tell you is that I will be faithful, dependable, and never be late."

He said, "That is what I am looking for."

At that point, I began to see the grace of God, and understanding His grace is a humbling experience. When he takes your life, anoints you, and makes you into something you never thought you could be, that is His grace in operation.

When I wrote *God's Armorbearer* [Tulsa: Harrison House, Inc., 1990], I was concerned that no one would ever read it. I wondered why God had asked me to write it, because I do not claim to be a writer.

When the first seven thousand and five hundred copies arrived, we stacked the boxes in a storage room. I closed the door, got down on my knees, and almost begged God to sell those books. It has been a real blessing to me to see God use

31

that book in the way that he has. Currently, it has remained a bestseller being sold worldwide in four languages.

You also have talents in your life that will come forth as you trust God's grace in the small things. We are what we are by His grace. If you always *obey* His original instructions, you will see things begin to work.

Many times, because of an over-zealousness to do great things for God, we start getting off the course He has set for us. We want to dream big dreams, and then go after those dreams. The problem with that is when you wake up one day and find out it was not God's dream but your own.

Following your own dream will lead to a dead-end street, usually with a lot of time and money wasted. You must stop and take a look at what God originally told you to do in the beginning. Go back to what He spoke to your heart. There is where you will find the peace of God and His prosperity.

Today it is easy for a Christian to say, "I feel led to do this," and "I feel led to do that." People move from one thing to another always "feeling led," but never Holy-Spirit-led.

A pastor told me once that he was so tired of having people come in his office saying "I feel led" that he was going to get a large chunk of lead to put on his desk. The next time someone said that, he was going to rub the lead and say, "So do I!"

If the Lord has told you to join a church and commit yourself there, then do exactly what He said. Determine to be the greatest blessing to your church that anyone ever has been. From there, God will direct you one step at a time, and you will not miss Him. We will not miss God, if we will learn to walk in the Spirit and stay with what God originally told us to do.

Patience and Flexibility

Patience is another key to longevity. Patience means "the suffering of afflictions, pain, toil, calamity, provocation or other evil with a calm, unfurled temper." Patience also means enduring without murmuring or fretting. Or it is the act, or quality, of waiting long for justice or expected good without discontent. Romans 12:6,7 says:

> **Having then gifts differing according to the grace that is given to us whether prophecy, let us prophesy according to the proportion of faith;**
>
> **Or ministry, *let us wait on our ministering*. . . .**

You can see where a lot of problems come from in our lives: We are not patient. We are not willing to endure hardships, and we always are looking for an opportunity to be personally exalted and promoted. The Bible says to *wait on our ministering*. God wants to develop His character in you first before He exalts your ministry. However, we usually like promotion first and character later.

As you determine to have the will of God operate in your life, and you get connected to a local church, the opportunities to murmur, complain, and become impatient will be there. Most of these feelings usually are directed to those in authority over us. We feel that *we* have a call and a place, and our pastors are not letting our gifts come forth.

That does happen occasionally, if you run into a pastor who is a controlling-type person. But, the bottom line even then is: Did God call you there? If He did, it probably was for the purpose of learning patience.

I have found that when I really want something to happen for me, when I really want a new door to open up, I first have to give it to the Lord. It is amazing that, when you do that, it will not be long until the door opens. You must relax in God and in ministry and let His perfect timing take place. It is by faith and patience that you will receive the promise.

Along with patience, you must have flexibility. That means *being willing to change*. We must be careful not to get in a rut. A rut is simply an elongated grave.

The majority of people in the world prefer to be "secure," which means keeping their own little "worlds" stable with little change. Because of this characteristic of human nature, we easily can get "tunnel vision" and miss the prompting of the Holy Spirit to make a change in our churches or in our lives.

If you look at what happened in the Church from the sixties right up to the present, you can see God moving in a different way in each decade.

In the sixties, God began to pour out His Spirit on all denominations and the Charismatic Movement resulted. The seventies brought a revival of the office of the teacher. Teaching centers began to spring up around the country. Then the eighties brought a new commitment and a call to emphasize local churches. Thus far in the nineties, the Lord has turned our attention to the harvest of the lost.

We can see from this how the Holy Spirit changes direction, and you can see why we need to follow His leading to get located for this last-day harvest. If you are going to be in the move of God, you must find out where He is moving and follow Him.

In your church, you will face many opportunities to change, and the changes may come in a way that will require time for you to adjust. In order for us and our churches to grow, we must be open to search our own hearts and let changes perfect us.

I believe God is challenging us to take steps of faith that we have never taken before. God wants to move us out of our comfort zones. The purpose is to open your ministry to reach more people. The children of Israel had it made as long as God put a cloud over them during the day to protect them from the desert sun, a fire at night to warm them, and manna to feed them.

At least, they had it made until God said it was time to change. He told them to possess the promised land. But He was going to take away their "securities," and they were going to have to fight and take the land by faith. What happened? They rebelled in unbelief. Why? It was time to make changes, and they were comfortable just the way they were.

Your life and ministry will stop dead in its tracks if you do not accept change. You will never accomplish what God has for you if you get comfortable. If you are going to reach out and minister to this generation, you will never do it with a sixties, seventies, or eighties mentality. You may be more comfortable with the way things were, but this generation thinks differently.

The Church must get with God and find out His strategies for reaching this generation. The ministries that do this are the ones that will move into the harvest years ahead of us.

3

Keys to Commitment

The first key to commitment is *a loyalty and faithfulness* that goes beyond *all* personal feelings. The dictionary defines *loyalty* as being "faithful to a prince or a superior, true to a plighted (vowed or sworn to) faith, duty, or love." Faithfulness is defined as "firmly adhering to duty, loyal, true to one's allegiance," or as being "a faithful subject."

These definitions show the heart of an armorbearer. This is someone willing to give of himself for others. He is dependable and loyal to his leaders and can be trusted with difficult assignments. Loyalty and faithfulness, of course, are first to God and then to man.

The Prophet Daniel and the three Hebrew children refused to eat the rich food usually served to the king's table when they were taken captive to Babylon. A lot of the food was totally against the dietary laws given to Moses by God. I have wondered why the other young captives did not follow their example.

When you think about it, however, you can hardly blame them. Their country had been destroyed, their family members probably all killed or least also held captive, and they were prisoners in a strange city. Perhaps they thought God had forsaken them and there no longer was reason to hold onto His laws. But Daniel remained faithful, and as a result, he was highly exalted in the middle of an ungodly nation.

Today, as a staff member of a church or ministry, when you are asked by a pastor or church leader to do something or change something, you are not a prisoner in an alien land as was Daniel. Your attitude to those over you is a test of your loyalty to God.

Loyalty always is tested first where God is concerned. If you do not like something a superior asks you to do, you may think it is between you and him. But it is really between you and God, if you are where God has put you. Make changes in your attitude and in your obedience to God, and then doing what you are asked to do will not bother you.

Personal feelings must be laid aside when you make a decision to serve God in whatever ministry He puts you. After all, He knew all of the rules and regulations of that ministry before He put you there.

Faithfulness is something that has to be found, according to 1 Corinthians 4:2. The Bible says to know those who labor among you. That is why your pastor and church leaders watch for faithfulness. When they find someone who has proven himself trustworthy in hard and difficult situations, they know that person is mature and can handle more responsibility.

Take a look at four characteristics of a faithful man:

1. A faithful man knows how to keep his mouth shut. (Prov. 11:13.)

2. A faithful man ministers strength to his pastor and church. (Prov. 13:17.)

3. A faithful man always will speak the truth. (Prov. 14:5.)

4. A faithful man is a humble man. (Prov. 20:6.)

No one works in or is a member of a perfect church. Nor are pastors perfect. It is hard to be faithful at times while working with imperfect people. On the other hand, if you examine your own life, you may find you are not as perfected as you think. But Jesus died on the cross for imperfect people, so we could all have divine life with Him. We are to give ourselves in the same way to bring people into the perfect Kingdom, which is God's.

Do Not Be Too Big or Too Small

Another key to commitment is: *Don't ever be too big to do the small, but don't ever be too small to do the big.* While teaching this to our staff that day, this point came from our Children's Minister. When he came on staff, he was called to work with children. He was very content and happy with what he was doing. But one day, he was asked to be on our children's TV program called, "Kids Like You."

Now this was all new to him. He thought, "There is no way I could ever be on TV and play a role as one of the main characters."

But God was stretching him to expand him into a new area for the purpose of reaching more children. It is always in God's plan to exalt you, but you will find you will have to expand. He had never once thought or desired to do that, but God had a plan. Sometimes we can miss God because we see more responsibility, and we are afraid we cannot handle it.

Now, on the other hand, we cannot get to the place that we are too big to do the small. There is an attitude in some leaders because of who they are that excuses them to do whatever they want and say whatever they want. But the Bible is very clear that they have a judge also.

There is a law that works for masters and servants alike — you reap what you sow. (Gal. 6:7.) Get lifted up by pride, and you are destined to fall. (Prov. 16:18.) If you are unteachable, you open the door to deception. Paul wrote that we should not think of ourselves more highly than we ought. (Rom. 12:3.) Once we begin to think we are better than others, problems begin. Determine to keep a humble heart and think soberly about yourself, and God will exalt you.

Another key to commitment is *committing to the ministry as you are committed to your marriage.* Of course, your marriage comes before your position in the church; however, you should approach the work for the Lord with the same fervency.

Concerning commitment, I heard a story of a farmer with a chicken and a pig who loved him because he was so good to them.

On the farmer's birthday, the chicken went to the pig and said, "Let's do something special for him," and the pig said, "That sounds great, but what can we do?"

The chicken said, "Let's serve him breakfast. I'll give him eggs, and you can give him bacon."

The pig said, "Wait a minute. You are only giving an offering, but you're asking *total commitment* out of me!"

It will require a total commitment to be faithful and do what you are called to do. The strongest key to having a successful marriage is communication. Likewise, in working with your pastor and leaders, communication is a must. The reason for misunderstandings is a lack of communication. Jesus always took the time to communicate with His disciples. He knew the continuation of His ministry depended on it.

This need for communication works both ways, of course. Workers need to let pastors and leaders know of potential problems, and pastors must take the time to put their hearts into their people. If a pastor is truly joined to his flock as a shepherd, the sheep will know his voice. A congregation of people cry for security. That comes from a commitment to a pastor, and that pastor making a commitment back to the people.

Always Do Your Best

Doing your best is another key to commitment. A pastor is always concerned about whether his staff and his congregation feel about the church the way he does. The way you can minister peace to him, as an armorbearer, is to always do your best.

A visitor walked into our church one morning with a crying child in her arms. The woman seemed upset, so one of our nursery workers took the child and told her to go on into the service. The woman made Jesus Lord of her life at the end of the service. That nursery worker saw a situation and did her best to help. When she stands before Jesus, she has a great reward waiting.

Colossians 3:23,24 says to do whatever you do heartily as unto the Lord and not unto men in order to receive the reward of the inheritance.

The final two keys to commitment:

1. *Stay with something until the job gets done.*

2. *Never quit or give up.*

If you are working in any department in a church, and you are given a job to do — just do it! Then, make sure it is completely finished. Many times we want to start a new project before the last one is finished.

You will have many opportunities to quit. They present themselves often. It takes no effort to quit; that is the easy way out. When God told me to be my pastor's armorbearer, no exceptions were included.

When we began to build the present church building, the Lord said to construct it "debt-free." Making a decision like that means a lot of work depends on the voluntary efforts of staff and congregation. It meant work days every Saturday. And, when we moved from the shopping center store-front church to the new building, it had no ceiling, no carpet, and an echo problem that was unbelievable.

Chairs had to be set up before every service and taken down afterwards, along with all of the sound and band equipment. Construction crews would come in the day after a service and make a huge mess. The floors would be covered in dust, so they had to be swept before every service. At times, we may have looked as if we were covered with a "glory cloud," but it was really sheet-rock dust.

When we began, we had plenty of volunteers, but as the weeks and months passed, it seemed only a few were left to help. It was my responsibility to make sure it was done. During this time, there were not many days to just relax. But I look back at it and would not trade that time for anything — although I am glad it is over. The "hardship" pulled things out of me that I did not know were there. Some were good, and some not so good. But through it, I learned the only way to succeed is never to quit.

When the carpet was finally laid, I got down on my knees and kissed it! That was the most beautiful sight I think I have ever seen.

If you are truly committed to the church and pastor where God has sent you, then you will not quit when you face hard times. The reality is that you will face challenges in the growth of your church that will test your commitment, whether you are a member or a pastor.

You will have the privilege of dealing with pride, anger, bitterness, selfishness, and all the destructive things that are in human behavior. But, once you learn to deal with these, overcome them, and let God begin a work in you, then you will become more like Him.

God is preparing you for leadership. The key is to stay committed to God, your call, and the leaders set over you.

4
Keys to Attitude

The first key to attitude is *a willingness to do whatever you are asked*. This is what leaders look for in people who desire to get involved. This is an attitude we all must develop in our hearts when we work in the Kingdom of God. You may not think you have the talent or ability to do whatever is asked, but you will set yourself to do it *because* you were asked.

Not long after coming to this church, I was asked to take care of the weekly bulletin. I have no artistic ability. The last time I did anything with art was pasting valentines in the fifth grade! But I told Pastor Caldwell I would be happy to do it. It took me a while, but I did it to the best of my ability because the church needed it done. Later, someone else came along with the necessary talent and took over that job.

Another time, I asked someone to help me with something, but that person said, "I'm sorry, but that is not my 'grace' gift."

That may have been so, but I was asking for help — not a word from God. However, that is the kind of attitude many people have in local churches, and that is why they are never used. What is on the inside of a person is more important than what is on the outside. The greatest blessing to me is when people come and say they are joining our church and want to know where they can help. Those are the people who end up in leadership positions.

The next key to the right attitude is *never lose sight of the people behind the work*. This thought came from one of our computer operators, who sits day after day keying information for the ministry into our computers. She said the Lord has helped her not to just type in name after name, but to be concerned about these people and to pray for them. You must not let what you do in the church turn into just another job.

Church workers must get a revelation of the people involved. They must know that they are working for *people,* loving *people,* and daily giving their lives for *people,* all of whom God loves. Without people, there would be no churches. People are the reason we are called to work in the Kingdom.

For example, it takes a lot of work to get ready for our annual Campmeeting. Sometimes, the best feeling about Campmeeting is when it is over! But, that was a wrong attitude, and it came because I let myself get caught up in all of the work and responsibility. My focus was not on people.

I am sure there were times when the disciples felt the same way, perhaps after Jesus fed thousands of men with loaves and fishes, not counting the women and children. When those meals were over and the leftovers gathered up in baskets, I expect that the disciples were glad. But, just think, they had a part in a wonderful miracle.

That is what you must always think: "Here is an opportunity to minister to more people, and God is letting me have a part."

If you get upset at all of the work you have to do, then you need to judge your heart's attitude. You are losing sight of the *people.* All of that work is changing people's eternal destiny, so it is worth it.

Be Thankful in All Things

A third key to having the right attitude is *being thankful for your position and retaining your joy.* We should always be thankful for the place in which God has put us. The Apostle Paul wrote that we should give thanks in everything, because it is the will of God for us. (1 Thess. 5:18.) You may want a change in your life and position, but that will only come when you learn to be thankful for where you are. We are not just to be thankful in good times, but even during difficult times.

I learned a valuable lesson on being thankful when I visited a missionary couple from our church living in northern Romania. The lifestyle there is like going back in time a hundred years in this country. This couple must do all of their cooking and baking by hand, and they have five children.

While there, they are responsible for raising up a church and a Bible School. For the first four months, they had no hot water, and when they finally got a hot water tank, it broke after working a while. Then it took several weeks to get it fixed.

Watching things that went on, I asked, "How do you make it?" They looked at me and spoke a revelation to my heart when they said, "We have learned to be thankful. If we have no *hot* water, then we thank God for any water at all. We pray in the Spirit one hour a day, and then we thank God continually."

That is an attitude that will cause you to win in any situation. The victory begins in thanksgiving.

Paul wrote in Phillippians 1:15-19 of some people who were preaching from the wrong heart with the purpose of adding afflictions to Paul, who was in prison at the time. But he did not develop the wrong attitude in return. Instead, he rejoiced over the fact that Christ was at least being preached.

If you have problems now in your ministry or work, begin to rejoice. That will bring you strength, and your strength will minister to everyone around you. You will have to fight to keep it, but it is yours. Joy is not determined by circumstances.

Paul learned that lesson years before when he and Silas were beaten with "many stripes" and cast into prison with their feet fastened in the stocks. But they prayed and sang praises to God, even at midnight, and there was a great earthquake which shook the foundations of the prison. The doors were opened, and everyone's bands were loosed. (Acts 16:23-26.)

Take a close look at the faith they exercised. Their backs were bleeding, they had been put in stocks, and all this for doing God's will. What a golden opportunity to complain and murmur. In the natural, if they were going to complain, this was the time to start. But, instead, they began to worship God.

I personally believe that Paul might have looked at Silas and asked how he was doing. In response, Silas said, "I'm in pain, but I'm going to make it."

Then Paul said, "Silas, let's do something that is probably the most ridiculous thing you have ever heard of at a time like this. Let's start praising God."

I am sure Silas said, "Paul, you're right. That is the most ridiculous thing I have ever heard. But, let's do it in faith, I'm with you."

I can imagine Jesus looking at the Father and saying, "Do You hear Our servants Paul and Silas giving Us praise? I know they are in pain, and I know they are suffering for My cause, but listen to their faith."

And God was so moved that He sent an earthquake, and *everyone's* bands were loosed. If you need doors to open, then begin to worship God and thank Him for Who He is. From that kind of praise will come deliverance for you, which will effect those around you. Hebrews 13:15

says we are to offer the sacrifice of praise continually, which is the fruit of our lips giving thanks.

A Servant's Heart Makes a Good Attitude

The next key to having a good attitude is *having a servant's heart*. Jesus told the disciples that, in the Kingdom of God, those who are "chief" are those who serve. He told them that He was among them as One who served. (Luke 22:25-27.) Jesus had a true servant's heart. Christians will never graduate from being servants.

Look at the life of Elisha, who began his ministry by acting as a servant for Elijah for a number of years. When Jehosophat, king of Judah, asked if there was not a prophet in the nation of Israel to go to for advice from the Lord, Elisha was named. However, it was not the miracles he had done or his powerful anointing that was mentioned. (2 Kings 3:10-12.)

A servant of the King of Israel said, "Here is Elisha, the son of Shaphat, *who poured water on the hands of Elijah.*"

In other words, it was his role as servant to a great man that was his recommendation. Elisha was Elijah's armorbearer.

That phrase "who poured water over Elijah's hands" became real to me when I visited Mike Croslow, one of our missionaries in Uganda. He took me out in the bush to preach in a village where there was no running water or electricity. It was not the end of the world, but you felt it was visible from that place!

We preached under a mango tree to hundreds of people and had a wonderful time. When it was time for lunch, we went into a small mud church and sat down at a table. I did not see any utensils, so I asked Mike if there were any.

He said, "No, brother, you get the honor of eating with your hands."

Then a young boy of about fourteen carried in a pitcher of water and a bar of soap. As the guest, he came to me first, handed me the soap and began to pour water over my hands. Then he continued around the room to all of the other ministers who were there. After that, food was brought in, and we prayed and ate. When we finished, the young man came back and poured water again to wash our hands.

After that experience, I understood better the culture of the Middle East in the days of Elijah and Elisha. The younger man would prepare the prophet's meal, bring water and pour it over Elijah's hands before he ate and after. He kept his house, did the cooking, and all of the other menial tasks required. Elisha truly had a servant's heart.

As you learn to serve, the anointing of God will increase on your life to help others. David became king and had a great anointing, but he first experienced God while tending sheep. He was willing to give his life to protect his father's sheep.

He watched that flock with a servant's heart and a watchful eye. You do not hear him complaining about having to take care of some stinking sheep. Because he passed the test of serving with the sheep, he was able to pass the test of Goliath when it came.

Now, what is *your* flock? Is it watching a group of toddlers every Sunday morning? Is it directing a choir, youth group, or children's church? Are you involved in housecleaning, door greeting, or ushering?

Your flock, or area of responsibility, is your "proving ground." If you function well as a servant, you will be promoted.

That brings us to a related key, which is to *serve as if you were serving Jesus*. From the Word of God, you can see clearly that the Bible says we are to work as if we are working for Jesus. If you will get your eyes off your boss and strive to please God first, then you will please your boss. We must learn to see Jesus as our Eternal Employer.

Understanding Authority

Servants, obey in all things your masters according to the flesh; not with eyeservice, as menpleasers; but in singleness of heart, fearing God:

And whatsoever ye do, do it heartily, as to the Lord, and not unto men.

Colossians 3:22,23

If Jesus asked you to clean the church bathrooms, how clean would they be?

If Jesus asked you to drive a bus on the church bus route, would you be on time?

If Jesus asked you to help in the church nursery, how well would you handle and treat the children?

If Jesus asked you to pray for your church and leadership, how fervently would you pray?

If Jesus asked you to get involved in your local church, how quickly would you respond?

When you volunteer and are asked to do something, you need to remember that it is as if Jesus Himself asked you, because you are doing whatever you do for Him.

This leads us to the attitude of *submitting to God's delegated authority in our lives*. Romans 13:1,2 says that authority is ordained of God and whoever resists authority is resisting God.

God established all authority in chains of command under Him. On this earth, from world governments to church governments, obedience to higher authority is ordained by God. Heaven is run under a principle of authority: God the Father, God the Son, and God the Holy Spirit, then the archangels, cherubs and seraphims, who are submitted to authority over them.

Now, if Michael the archangel tells an angel to go take care of a situation on earth, that angel does not say, "But I only take orders from Gabriel." He would never do that, because he remembers very clearly what happened to the last groups of angels who acted that way.

All *offices* of authority are set up by God, and the authority rests on the office, not the man. We are to submit ourselves to the office, whether or not we like the man in the office. If he misuses his office, we can pray for him to change or pray him out.

In order to properly submit to authority, you must have a clear understanding that the authority rests in the office, not the man. If a president is voted out of office in this country, he no longer has authority in what goes on. A former president cannot just drive up to the White House and walk into the Oval Office without going through the proper security protocol than can the most ordinary citizen. Why? That is because he no longer is in authority.

When God told Moses to speak to the rock in Numbers 20:8-29, we see Moses and Aaron both in rebellion against what God had commanded. Moses angrily struck the rock instead of speaking to it, and Aaron stood with him in this rebellion. Well, God told Moses to bring Aaron and his son, Eleazar, to Mount Hor. There, Moses was instructed by God to take the high priest's robe off of Aaron and place it on Eleazar. When that happened, Aaron died. This shows us what happens when we misrepresent God before people. The authority on the high priest's office remained, but it was now on Eleazar.

When we submit to people and to authority, we submit to the office. The only right we have not to submit to authority is when that authority directly violates the Word of God. When we are asked to do something that is in direct violation of the Word of God, then we do not submit, because we have a *higher* authority.

But, let's be real honest, that is not usually the case. Rebellion usually starts when you have to submit to the rules in your church nursery. That is where it begins. Then it goes into the requirements of joining the church, and when you finally get through that, you are faced with what it takes to be an usher, door greeter, housekeeper, sing in the choir, play in the band, teach in Sunday school, and so on.

Another type of authority which plays a major part in many local churches is: *That is the way we do it around here.* Wherever you go, you will be faced with this "authority." And it does not matter whether you agree with the way things are done or not, you must submit if you know God wants you to be a part of that church or ministry.

If you get mad and begin to speak against the pastor and leaders, then you are in rebellion. You are not coming against the people in those offices; you are coming against God. If you have a problem with something, take the time and make the effort to go talk with the leadership in an attitude of love and let them explain why they operate the way they do.

Five Structures of Authority

There are five structures of authority that we all must submit to:

1. *God and His Word* (1 John 2:3,4)

We must keep God's Word in our hearts and fully submit to the laws laid down in the Word of God. The reason is that we will be judged according to the Bible, so our lives must line up with the Bible as God's Word.

2. *National and local government* (1 Pet. 2:13,14)

51

The Apostle Peter wrote that Christians must submit to *every* ordinance of man for the Lord's sake. For example, if you work, you must pay taxes and file with the Internal Revenue Service. Otherwise, you may go to jail. You may not like this, but you have to do it, because it is the law. If we rebel against paying those taxes, we really are rebelling against God and not man. On the other hand, if laws are passed forbidding us to preach, then the national laws have rebelled against God, and we have a higher authority to obey.

3. *The church*

One day in 1980, I was sitting in my office at the church reading my Bible, when I heard the Spirit of God say, "Have a Pastor's Appreciation Day."

I had never heard of such a thing. I was raised in church, but we never did anything like that. So I told the rest of the staff, and we worked it all out.

One Sunday morning, I walked into the pulpit, and you could see that Pastor Caldwell was wondering what in the world was going on. Then I announced it was Pastor's Appreciation Day, and we blessed him financially by receiving a special offering. Also, we had people come up and share what the Caldwells had meant to them.

Each year since, we have done this to let the pastor and his wife know that we love and appreciate them. However, several years ago, someone came to me who felt we were lifting up a man and not exalting Jesus. I searched my heart and the Bible and found 1 Timothy 5:17,18:

> **Let the elders that rule well be counted worthy of double honour, especially they who labour in the word and doctrine.**
>
> **For the scripture saith, Thou shalt not muzzle the ox that treadeth out the corn. And, The labourer is worthy of his reward.**

When I realized that the Bible said pastors are worthy of double honor, I realized we were on target. Pastors have authority and must give an account of that authority. They deserve appreciation. Hebrews 13:17 says:

Obey them that have the rule over you, and submit yourselves: for they watch for your souls, as they that must give account, that they may do it with joy, and not with grief: for this is unprofitable for you.

I want to challenge every staff member and every church member who reads this book to get together with others in your church and set aside a day to show your pastors that you love them. Pray and ask the Lord what He would have you do, and then bless them with the best you can. Do this once a year to encourage them. You will find that God will honor this, and the love of God will flow in your church.

4. *The family*

Paul wrote in Ephesians 6:1 for children to obey their parents in the Lord, *for this is right*. As long as you are living under the roof of your parents, you must submit to them. If you are over forty years old and still living with your mom and dad, then you will have to submit to them in many areas of your life. My suggestion is to move out. Once you are not living in their house, you are no longer under their authority. However, remember that the Bible says you are always to honor them.

5. *Employers*

Peter wrote that servants should be subject to their masters and not only to those masters who are "good and gentle." (1 Pet. 2:18.) That makes it very clear that we must submit on our jobs to whoever is in authority over us. That means to pray for your boss, and if they are harsh or demanding, pray that God will get hold of them and turn them into "gentle masters."

Stop complaining and start praying. Then make sure you are on time and do a good job. They will be ministered to by your diligence. If you do this, God will more than likely open a door for you to share Christ with them.

The centurion who told Jesus to just "speak the word" and his servant would be healed understood authority. The centurion was a man *in* authority. He also was a man *under* authority. Jesus said He had not found anyone in Israel with this kind of faith. Why did that Roman centurion have such faith? He *understood* authority. (Matt. 8:9.) He could tell that demons and disease were subject to the authority of Jesus.

In conclusion: *Authority is here to stay*. We will never graduate from under authority. When we get to heaven, we will still submit to authority. Those who climb God's ladder into spiritual authority and do exploits for Him are the ones who know how to submit and flow with authority. God will never exalt you into a greater place of authority until you learn how to submit to authority.

Reproof of Instruction Is the Way of Life

The last key to maintaining a good attitude is *being big enough to be rebuked and corrected*. Proverbs 6:23 says that "reproofs of instruction" are the way of life. We will be reproved and corrected in life, because we are human and make mistakes. If you want to mature, you must remain teachable.

> **Reprove not a scorner, lest he hate thee: *rebuke* a wise man, and he will love thee.**
> **Give *instruction* to a wise man, and he will be yet wiser: *teach* a just man, and he will increase in learning.**
> **Proverbs 9:8,9**

If you are one who is going to rebuke, then be wise enough to *instruct* and *teach*. I have seen people who felt called to "rebuke," but there was no teaching or instruction.

54

That kind of rebuke amounts to criticism and results in nothing but wounds and strife. God never assigned anyone to break a person's spirit. We are always to rebuke with meekness and love and take the time to teach the person how to do right and what they have done wrong.

On the other hand, if you are the one being rebuked, do not get your feelings hurt. Be big enough to take it and go on without holding a grudge and being defensive. It is very clear from the Word of God that a wise man will listen to correction, and judge himself. (Prov. 13:1.) A fool despises any instruction.

> **The way of a fool is right in his own eyes: but he that hearkeneth unto counsel is wise.**
> **Proverbs 12:15**
>
> **He that refuseth instruction despiseth his own soul: but he that heareth reproof getteth understanding.**
> **Proverbs 5,10,32**
>
> **Smite a scorner, and the simple will beware: and reprove one that hath understanding, and he will understand knowledge.**
> **Proverbs 19:25**

I must admit that I have met some fools in my life. They will not take any correction. Their shortcomings and problems were always someone else's fault. They are always right. What do you do with people like that? You stay away from them and watch what happens to them. They will never fulfill God's will, because they will not admit mistakes.

We are told in the Bible to judge ourselves and make corrections when we need to change. If you refuse to judge yourself, you will face judgment on the sin in which you live.

I believe it is very important today to have people around us to whom we are accountable, people who can speak into our lives. That is why the Bible says to submit to

God-called leadership, so they can help us if we begin to miss it. We cannot afford to miss the will of God in our lives.

Stay humble before the Lord, and when you are corrected or rebuked, receive it and learn from it. Then you will grow into the place God intends for you to be. There is no growth without some pruning. God wants fruit to come forth in your life and remain.

5

Keys to Teamwork

I want to begin this chapter with something the Holy Spirit quickened to me, and that is an analogy between an NFL football team and the operation of the local church.

People involved and points to remember

I. **Coaches in the press box.** They see the overall field, and they see the way the defense is set up. They can tell by this which play is the best to call, and they are the ones who call the plays. Their job is to watch the defense to spot any weakness, then quickly call a play to take advantage of it.

This is the **Father and the Son of God**, Who sit in the press box and call the plays. They know the devil's tactics and defenses and which play will work against them. Paul wrote that we should not let Satan take advantage of us, for we are not ignorant of his devices. (2 Cor. 2:11.)

There are three heavens in the universe. (2 Cor. 12:2.) The first heaven is over the earth where we live, the second is the realm where Satan, demons, and angels dwell, and the third heaven is where God's throne is. The Bible makes it clear that Satan is the prince and power of the air. God looks down on the second heaven and sees clearly the defense of the devil against the church.

He then calls down to the Coach on the playing field and communicates to him what the devil is doing, so he can then let the quarterback know what play to run.

The coaches in the press box will always make a video tape of every play, so they can take a look at the last play while another play is being run on the field. That way they can analyze the defense and see what the opposing team is setting up. Our Father has the ability to see past, present, and future. He knows the right play to call every time. It is up to us to listen to the **Coach on the field of play**.

II. **The coach on the field.** He assists in calling the plays, but his most important job is to communicate those plays to the quarterback. He is there to encourage and strengthen the team's confidence. He never leaves the field until the game is over.

The Coach on the field for the Church, of course, is the **Holy Spirit.** He is the Head Coach on the field of play with us. (John 16:7.) He is always encouraging us when we get tired or hurt. He will be with us until the game is over.

When a player is discouraged with his performance, the Coach begins to build up his confidence. He will tell that player that he *is* going to make it, he can win this game. That is the Word of the Holy Spirit to us. We can make it, we can win, we are the Lord's very best, and nothing is impossible with God on our side.

The Holy Spirit will only speak or call the plays that he hears from the Father. (John 16:13.) Then He communicates those directions to the quarterback.

III. **The Quarterback.** He is the head communicator on the playing field. He must effectively call the plays given to him by the coaches. He must run the offense. He depends fully on the coaches to spot the weaknesses in the defense in order to win the game. The quarterback must be healthy and strong in order to win the game. No team can win without a good quarterback.

This is the **Pastor**. He must call the play for the team. He must depend on the Holy Spirit to give orders and follow His instructions. Running the right play and gaining yards will come by being obedient to the Head Coach, the Holy Spirit.

As any head coach runs his team a little different from any other, so will the Holy Spirit run each local church in a different way. What works for one will not always work for another.

The Holy Spirit wants the pastor to hear the plays from Him. After the pastor has received the play, he must effectively communicate it to the team in order for the play to work. Many plays have failed and penalties resulted, because the players did not know the play or on what count the ball was to be snapped.

Pastors must also hand the ball off to the other "backs," so that their abilities and talents can be used in gaining yards for the team. Any quarterback understands the gifts and talents that are there to assist the team.

In our analogy, the "football" is the vision, and it must be handed to the other staff ministers, so that they can "make yardage." If a pastor hangs onto the vision because of insecurity, he will hinder the team. No quarterback can win the game by himself.

In fact, if a head coach sees a quarterback refusing to hand off or throw the football to another player, he will discipline him and take him out of the game if he does not make the adjustments. The most valuable person on the team is the quarterback, who controls the offense. But the quarterback knows his success depends fully upon those around him.

Points to remember:

A. No quarterback can win the game by himself. The other players must do their jobs in order to gain yards. Quarterbacks have been frustrated, bruised, hurt, and even knocked out of the game due to a lineman who let his defensive man through the line. Each player must do his job in order for the team to win.

B. The quarterback cannot do the job of a tackle just as a tackle cannot do the job of a quarterback. Each is gifted in his place. All must carry the same vision, and that is to score and to win the game.

C. Every quarterback must take time for a huddle. In the huddle, he calls the plays so each person knows his assignment for that down.

III. **Halfbacks, Fullbacks, and Ends.** They, along with the quarterback, must advance the ball. They must be strong, quick, and creative in making the right moves. They must not be concerned about which back is making the most yards. If one is having a good game, then *give him the ball*. The goal is to win the game, and not be concerned with who is scoring. These players, like the quarterback, will receive the majority of the recognition due to their special gifts and talents.

Once they receive the ball, it is up to them to think quickly and creatively in order to move it down the field. They depend on the linemen to clear the way for them. The first thing they must do is take the ball from the quarterback. Fumbles are caused by not remembering the basics.

These are the **Associate Ministers**. They are gifted by God to run with the vision and effectively communicate it to the people. They have the freedom to think creatively, but must remember to listen to the play the pastor calls, then take the hand off.

No halfback or fullback will call the play; it is always the quarterback. The different backs have the right to tell the quarterback that they are open, or that they know they can break through the line. But it is still up to the quarterback to call the play.

If the associates take the hand off from the pastor, then run in an opposite direction of the play, there will be major problems. They must go in the direction of the team. Just as a quarterback will be set down by the head coach if he does not listen to the play, so will the associates be set down by their pastors and the Holy Spirit if they try to do their own thing.

Creativity comes once they are running with the ball (vision). They must realize that once they have scored, it was a team effort and not theirs alone. Many a football player has become lifted up in pride thinking he alone was the reason his team won. Associates depend on the office staff and those in the ministry of helps to clear obstacles out of the way in order for their gifts to have the opportunity to come forth. Gifted athletes are stopped on the scrimmage line when the linemen are unable to do their jobs.

IV. **The Linemen.** They are the backbone and work horses of the offense. Their jobs are to protect the quarterback and clear the way for the backs to make yardage. They must listen to every play called and for the snap count, even though they are tired or hurt. They must have a great tolerance for pain. Linemen do not get a lot of fanfare but have great joy when their team scores. They are always the toughest and strongest on the team and must be determined that no defensive lineman is going to get through. Their attitudes are that no one sacks our quarterback or catches our backs behind the line.

This is the equivalent of the **Office Staff and Ministry of Helps.** They are the backbone of a church. They must stay built up, have a winning attitude, and determination that no devil gets our pastor. They do not get most of the fanfare, but every pastor and associate knows they are nothing without these workers. Everyone shares in the victory.

They must listen carefully to the Pastor to know the direction in which the team is going. Joy comes from seeing souls born into the Kingdom because they did their jobs.

Teams win through unity, motivation for winning, determination, endurance, practice, and ability. These are all true in the ministry. When one scores, we all score. When one wins, the whole team wins. At the end of the Superbowl, all the players on the winning team receive rings and a big bonus check. No matter their position, each player receives the same prize. As we are faithful to our positions, we — like Superbowl champs — will receive from God the same reward because we did the job He called us to do and we won as a team.

I would like to discuss some keys to teamwork that are a must in fulfilling the vision of the local church.

Keys to Teamwork

The first key is *walking without offense*. The main reason why people leave churches is because they get offended. Instead of dealing with whatever was said or done, they harbor bitterness from offenses in their hearts and end up leaving their churches.

There was a documentary on TV recently on how Africans catch monkeys. Now a monkey is very intelligent, so the African had to do something to out think the animal. He first put a cage on the ground with a bright object inside it. The door to the cage was left open to tempt the monkey to go in. When he did, a trap was set on the door to cause it to close and catch him. But the monkey would not go into the cage.

So the Africans closed the cage and made the wire around the cage just big enough so the monkey could get his hand in the cage. Now, when the monkey saw the bright object, he put his hand through the wire and grabbed it, but could not get it out of the cage. With the object in hand, he could not pull it through. He could only be free if he would let go of the object. The African then took a club and knocked the monkey over the head, and it died. Now, you would think that the monkey would have been smarter than that.

Many who are backslidden today are like these monkeys. They reached into the devil's "cage" by taking hold of an offense and refuse to let go. He is hitting them over the head with sickness, strife, and all types of marriage, family and financial problems. They have given themselves over to bitterness, and it is destroying them.

All they have to do to be free and remain free of that trap is to *let go* of hurts and wounds. God can heal and restore a person immediately if he will forgive offenses and repent of bitterness. Some readers have been hurt by their pastors or church leaders and allowed that to build up. If you are leaving your church or have already left, *please stop!* Go to the pastor or the one who offended you, and ask him to forgive you. That is the only way you are going to have true peace in your heart and family.

Anyone can take offense, get hurt, and walk out, but it takes a real man or woman of God to make it right. There is no Biblical reason to hold a grudge or to live in resentment. And there is every reason not to. Matthew 18:34,35 says:

> **And his lord was wroth, and delivered him to the tormentors, till he should pay all that was due him.**
>
> **So likewise shall my heavenly Father do also unto you, if ye from your hearts forgive not *every one* his brother their trespasses.**

The next key to teamwork is *using all your talents and abilities*. The church must function like a team, and in order to do so, the team needs your talents and abilities. I believe you have talents lying dormant just waiting to be used. In the midst of being faithful where you are placed, begin to draw on the abilities in you. You have the Creator on the inside. Pray and trust Him for His complete will to be fulfilled in your life.

In Matthew 25, we find the Parable of the Talents as told by Jesus. Matthew 25:13,14 says:

Watch therefore, for ye know neither the day nor the hour wherein the Son of man cometh.

For the kingdom of heaven is as a man traveling into a far country, who called his own servants, and delivered them his goods.

Jesus was comparing the Kingdom of God to a man taking a far journey and calling his servants together. Now this shows us Jesus as the one taking the journey, and He has called you and me together and delivered unto us His goods. So each of us has received something from Jesus.

Matthew 25:15 says:

And unto one he gave five talents, to another two, and to another one; to every man according to his several ability; and straight way took his journey.

Jesus uses money as the example, but as you continue through Chapter 25, you find in verse 35 these words:

For I was an hungered, and ye gave me meat: I was thirsty and ye gave me drink.

This proves to us that He was not only referring to money, but also to us using the gifts and callings we have to help others. So I am going to use the word *talents* to refer to our gifts and callings. Jesus gave to one five talents, and to another two talents, and to another one. He then took his journey after He was raised from the dead and now has given to each of us certain talents to be used for His Kingdom.

You may say, "Brother Nance, I don't have any gifts, or talents."

But you do, according to 1 Peter 4:10, which says that Jesus gave us gifts from God. We have no choice in the matter; Jesus is the one who gave out the talents. So if you have two talents and someone else got five, it does no good to be jealous or complain.

God did not call me up before His throne before I was born and say to me, "Terry, I am now ready to allow you to be born in the earth, but before you go, which gifts would you like to take with you?"

I would say, "Well, Lord! Give me that Apostle gift and that Prophet gift, and while You're at it, throw in gifts of healing and working of miracles."

The bottom line is that each of us is only accountable for his own gifts and callings and not for someone else's. Matthew 25:19 tells us there will come a "reckoning day." Romans 14:10 says that we will all stand before the judgment seat of Christ.

I know personally I will not stand before God and give account to Him for the ability to play the drums. I cannot play the drums, because I have very little rhythm. So, if it is not there, then it is not there. But I do have other abilities that I can use to bless the Kingdom of God.

As you read verses 22 and 23, you find Jesus saying to the one who had received two talents the same thing he said to the first one to whom He gave the five talents. This proves to us that if we are faithful to do with what God has given us, we will all receive the same reward. God only holds you responsible for what He gave you. If I am faithful to do what God called me to do as a Senior Associate of Agape Church, and Pastor Caldwell is faithful to do what God calls him to do, then we will receive the same reward, because we were faithful with the gifts and callings we both received.

The Spirit of God is saying loud and clear that it is time for us to release our gifts. We do not want to be like the servant in the parable who received one talent and went and buried it. That man was called "a wicked and slothful" servant.

You are part of a team, and a chain is only as strong as its weakest link. So rise up and bind away fear and get rid of all hurt and offense and begin to do something for the Kingdom. God will begin to add gifts, as you release what you already have.

Do not be like the man who prayed, "God, use me! Use me!" then after working in the church for a while, he went back to the Lord and said, "Lord, I just feel used."

God Does Not Create "Throw-Aways"

The next key to teamwork is a major one: *Know that you are important and needed.* God never created anything to be discarded. In the world's system, we place great value on the things that are one of a kind. These are the items that are priceless. You must understand that God made you one of a kind, and you are a priceless gift to the Church.

When you take a close look at 1 Corinthians 12:12-25, you will see the importance of each part of the body. The Apostle Paul made a comparison of the physical body to the Body of Christ, and pointed out that the body has many members but all work as a team.

This is how the Body of Christ and the local churches should function. As you read those verses in which Paul points out that the eye cannot do without the hand, and vice versa, we can see that he is saying there should be no jealousy between "parts" of the Body.

Our hands, feet, eyes are all important parts of the physical body. We would look very funny if we were just one great big nose. Thank God, we are not made like that. You are what God made you in the Body of Christ, and you are a vital part. The key is your hooking up with the other parts and working together toward a common goal.

And Paul wrote that it was God Who set the members in the Body as it pleased Him. God made each of us unique and gave us qualities that no others possess exactly as we do. Every Christian has something valuable to God and to the Body. So, if I am called to function as a hand, then it is up to me to be the best hand that I can be. My gifts and talents please God, so I know that I am valuable to the team.

Paul pointed out that even the uncomely, or unseen, parts of the body are as important as the others. There is nothing beautiful about a liver, for example. But you must realize that you cannot live without one. I believe the inward, or uncomely, parts of the body represent the ministry of helps. They are always in the background working, but you do not see them that much.

I have heard teachers refer to those in the ministry of helps as being in a lower position or as "playing second fiddle" in the Body. That grieves my spirit, and I believe it also grieves the Holy Spirit. In their function, the ministry of helps are just as important to God as the five-fold ministry gifts.

A great evangelist told about dreaming of standing before the judgment seat of Christ. There on a table were all types of crowns, but in the middle was a huge crown decked out with jewels, by far the most beautiful of all.

He stood there and thought, "That must be my crown, for I have won millions to Christ."

Finally an angel called his name and picked up a small crown right next to the big one for him. The evangelist stopped the angel and asked if he knew who he was and that he had won millions to Jesus.

But the angel said, "Yes, but this is the right crown." He was sad and a little distraught over receiving a small crown.

Then a little elderly woman's name was called out, and she went up to have the large, beautiful crown placed on her head. So the evangelist immediately wanted to know who she was, and the angel said, "This is the woman who faithfully prayed for you."

He received a revelation that God said more abundant honor sometimes is bestowed on those that we think to be less important. (1 Cor. 12:22-24.)

If you are going to fulfill your part in the Body, you must stop looking at your inabilities and start using your abilities. Get connected with the other parts, be faithful to your local church, and begin to run with the vision of the church

Run With the Vision

In Acts 4, we are told of the disciples being threatened for praying in Jesus' name. They got together with the brethren and began to pray, and when they had prayed, the house where they were was shaken. They were all filled with the Holy Spirit and spoke God's Word with boldness.

Acts 4:32 makes a very important point. The "multitude of them that believed" were all of *one heart and one soul*. In other words, they were in agreement. That is the key to seeing a great shaking of the Holy Spirit in our churches and cities. We are all of one heart when we are born again, because we all belong to Jesus. But are we all "one soul"?

A corporate anointing came on them, because they were in unity. They all had the same vision: to take the Gospel to the world no matter the personal cost. They were determined to flow together, recognize the authority of the apostles, and follow what Jesus was saying through them.

God speaks the vision into the heart of a local pastor, and that vision must get inside of the believers. Then they are to run in heart and soul toward the fulfillment of it. A corporate anointing on a local church will impact a city.

What is the vision of your local church? What is God saying through your pastor? Take hold of that vision and begin to run with your pastor, heart and soul. It is the plan and will of God that you flow with your pastor's heart and soul. Paul prayed for the Corinthians to *all speak the same thing* and have no divisions among them. (1 Cor. 1:10.)

If you are trying to run with a vision that God has not given your pastor, then you are going to create division. You need to stop and hook into what God is saying to your pastor and begin running in the same direction.

Do you really want to do exploits for God? Are you willing to find your place in the Body and get connected with the other members of your local church? Are you ready to release the gifts and talents God has put in you? If so, begin by becoming involved. God will never force Himself on you. He gives you the right to choose. But think what can be accomplished for God's Kingdom when you begin to do your part.

We are called to be armorbearers one for another. That commitment is a lifetime responsibility. Now is the time to pick up your spiritual sword and join the ranks of God's great army. We will stand victorious together because where one will put a thousand to flight, two will put ten thousand to flight.

The last and final key to teamwork is to *rest in God, and let Him lead you into the perfect plan for your life.* You must learn to trust God and let Him bring to pass the course laid out in His mind for you. We should not lean to our own understanding. (Prov. 3:5,6.) God is the one who directs our paths.

While attending Rhema in 1979, the Lord instructed us to resign from a church where we were working and just attend another one. Then, for the first time in my life, I was faced with no requirements to be at church. However, Kim and I made sure we were there three or four times a week.

I went to work part time at a shoe store, and Kim worked as a private sitter for elderly people in a nursing home.

Every day for seven or eight months, I went to work ten minutes early to sit in the car and speak out these words:

"I have a call on my life, and I am not going to sell shoes and smell feet for the rest of my life. When I get out of this car, Lord, I thank you that I am walking into the ministry where I am working fulltime."

We believed God in every area of our lives, especially in the financial area. Kim would tell the old people she took care of about Jesus. They would get saved, but because they were so old, they would die. As long as they were alive, Kim got paid. When they died, she had no job!

I went over to the nursing home and declared to them, "You will live and not die" — but they died anyway. I asked Kim why she always got the hopeless cases to look after. Why didn't they assign her someone who had some life in them?

Three weeks before school was out that year, another lady Kim was helping died. Then my boss came in and said the shoe business was being taken over in three weeks by his son, and he did not need me. There we were with neither of us having jobs and no prospect of joining a church staff.

All the churches we contacted wanted to know was whether my wife played the piano and sang. Well, she sang, but could not play the piano, so they would say, "Sorry. We need someone with talent."

I began to think, "Dear Lord, I could be the biggest jerk around and I could be a thief, but if my wife could play the piano, I could make it in the ministry!"

I was so down one night that I lay on the floor of our apartment and cried my eyes out. I had the biggest "pity party" I had ever had. In the middle of this, suddenly Jesus interrupted my party. His voice was so clear.

He said, "Son, why are you crying? Don't you realize I am up here interceding for you?"

That shook me to my toes. I jumped up and began to shout and dance and praise God for His mercy. I did not know how He would do it, but I was then sure that He did have a plan for my life.

The next Sunday morning at church, a young man came up to me whom I had never met. He had met my mother and seen a picture of me when he visited my parents' church in Arkansas. He was not looking for me, but that morning he just "happened" to sit a few seats away from me and recognized me. He asked me to lunch.

Three weeks later, we graduated from Rhema and decided to move back to my home town of Magnolia, Arkansas, where I could work in my brother's shoe store. When we arrived at my parents' home, however, my brother said he could not use me. Things were not getting any better fast.

Before leaving Tulsa, we had received one invitation to hold a small seminar in Florida. Right before we were to leave, the young man who had introduced himself to us at church in Tulsa called and told us about Pastor Happy Caldwell. He had just started a church in Little Rock and was looking for some people to help him. The young man asked if I would be interested in meeting with Pastor Caldwell. Needless to say, I did not need to look at my ministry calendar, because I did not have one.

So after we got back from Florida, we went to Little Rock. There were many other divine connections that God brought about along the way to get my wife and me hooked up with the Caldwells to help them with their vision of reaching Little Rock for Jesus.

You see, God is the best "chess player" there ever will be. He knows how to put you where He wants you. You may find yourself some place and not understand why, but if you trust God, you will see in the end that He was working out His divine plan.

In this book, I have shared some of the many challenges in my life as examples of those that will come when you are in the will of God. But He has delivered us out of them all. He orchestrated events in our lives to plant us where He wanted. It has been here that God has caused us to *Bloom Where We Have Been Planted.*

Many are called, but few are chosen. Stepping into that place of the chosen of God comes by prayer, faith, integrity, diligence, and excellence of ministry. You must determine to have those in your life and be committed to the will of God no matter the cost.

All of us are God's armorbearers, marching forward to serve in this earth, to do our parts in evangelizing the nations. Let us not be weak in faith and wander in our callings any longer. Let us do what our hands find to do, serve our God-called leaders, and pray in the last-day move of the Holy Spirit.

This is *our* generation, *our* day and hour, and *our* time to rise up and be the lights God wants us to be. We are God's army, God's voice, God's instrument in the earth: *We are the Local Churches.*

ABOUT THE AUTHOR

Humorously stating that he has been an active member of the local church for 46 years, the day after he was born, **Terry Nance** has actually been preaching the Word of God since the age of 13. Licensed by the Assemblies of God at age 20, Terry attended Southwestern Assemblies of God Bible College in Waxahachie, Texas, where he graduated with a Bachelor of Science. In 1978, Terry attended and graduated from Rhema Bible Training Center in Tulsa, Oklahoma. It was here while praying in an empty field, that Terry received his calling to the nations through a vision from the Lord.

Entering the full-time ministry in 1979 under the leadership of Pastor Happy Caldwell, Terry served as Senior Associate Minister of Agape Church in Little Rock, Arkansas for 23 years. While there, Terry also pioneered the Agape School of World Evangelism (ASWE), a daily full-time Bible school focused on training men and women to go in the power of the Word and the Spirit, revolutionizing the nations with the gospel of Jesus Christ. As the full-time Bible school grew, Terry also developed a weekly Laymen's School and a full-time evening ASWE Bible school. As Executive Director of ASWE, Terry also became the Executive Director of the Agape Belize International Training Center in Central America where potential missionaries were stationed for cross-cultural training. Reproducing a spirit of excellence and integrity, the graduating students from Terry's leadership continue to revitalize the nations for God by raising up schools and churches in nations such as Belize, England, Mexico, Philippines, Sweden, Finland, Norway, Romania, Iceland, India, Scotland and Niger. In his passion to see the nations saturated with the gospel, Terry also pioneered and became the Executive Director of the Agape Missionary Alliance, a program designed to help local churches in the funding, equipping and sending of missionaries.

During this time, Terry authored two books, *God's Armorbearer I: How to Serve God's Leaders*, and *God's Armorbearer II: Bloom Where You Are Planted*. On the publisher's best-selling list for the past 10 years, these books have motivated thousands of Christians to stand with their leaders in faithful service, helping to fulfill God's vision for the nations. In organizations and churches throughout the world, leaders and pastors continue to make these two books required reading for their people and their ministry staffs.

In 2002, Terry received a personal mandate from the Lord to begin his own ministry. Based on the words of Jesus in John 4:35, *Focus on the Harvest, Inc.* was birthed. As Founder and President, Terry has now committed his life to travel to local congregations throughout the nations and awaken believers to this strategic generation. Through his God-given passion and revelation, believers are ignited to discover their individual gifts and callings, commit to the vision of their local church and focus on the harvest of souls throughout their city, state, nation and world.

An important segment of *Focus on the Harvest, Inc.* is the *Armorbearer Leadership School.* Based on Terry's two books, God's Armorbearer I & II, this vital one day school is taught in four sessions, with the sole purpose of helping pastors to fulfill their visions and build their churches for the harvest. Through it, Terry imparts lasting truths such as why it's important to stand beside the pastor, how to run with and support the vision of the pastor, how to flow with the personality of the leadership, and how to know the difference between "the anointing" and "the human side" of leadership. The *Armorbearer Leadership School* awakens the gifts and talents of the people, enabling them to take their place within the vision of their local church. It is designed to increase the spiritual atmosphere of the local church, increase the participation in the pastor's vision and increase the commitment and loyalty of the people.

Terry and his wife Kim, have been married over 25 years. Kim also attended Southwestern Assemblies of God Bible College and graduated from Rhema Bible Training Center and Agape School of World Evangelism. A passionate and accomplished teacher of the Word, Kim frequently travels the nations, also helping to establish and strengthen churches and Bible schools. Terry and Kim reside in Arkansas and are the parents of three children, McCall, Alex and McKenna. Their daughter McCall, now in her mid-teens, has already traveled the nations assisting veteran missionaries in their work.

Terry's newest book releases, *Vision of the House* and *The Armorbearer Study Guide* will be released in 2003. Write to Terry Nance at *Focus on the Harvest, Inc.* for further information on how to obtain tapes, videos and materials that will enhance your church and increase your revelation for the harvest of souls in America and the nations of the world.

To contact the author for *Armorbearer* materials such as tapes and videos, for additional materials by Terry Nance, or to schedule an *Armorbearer Leadership School* in your church or area, write or call:

Terry Nance
Focus on the Harvest, Inc.
P.O. Box 6655
Sherwood, AR 72124
(501) 753-0033

www.godsarmorbearer.com
tnance@focusontheharvest.com

Additional copies of
this book and
God's Armorbearer, I
are available from
your local bookstore.

In Canada contact:
Word Alive
P. O. Box 670
Niverville, Manitoba
Canada ROA 1EO